Praise for *Death Is a Day Worth Living*

"Ana Claudia is a clear and compassionate guide on a journey into a daunting yet essential topic. Her powerful storytelling reminds us that the beauty of each day is heightened by our willingness to see suffering and mortality as an essential part of living. This book has the potential to change both your life and death."

—**Roy Remer,** executive director of Zen Hospice Project, San Francisco

"This engaging book is a celebration of life that springs from looking clearly and squarely at death. Through her deep humanity at the bedside of countless patients facing the end of life, Dr. Ana Claudia Quintana Arantes shares moving stories that reveal the profound truth that even in the face of terminal illness there is always something to be done. This book is a must-read for anyone living with a serious illness and for anyone serious about living life fully."

—**Dr. Steven Pantilat,** professor of medicine; chief of the division of palliative medicine at the University of California, San Francisco; author of *Life after the Diagnosis: Expert Advice on Living Well with Serious Illness for Patients and Caregivers*

"*Death Is a Day Worth* Living addresses a universal need for language around the one experience we will all go through—death. Until we take our last breath, we are very much alive, if we choose to be. Ana Claudia powerfully and poetically speaks to the privilege of being alive until the very end. This profound book reframes everyday life and everyday breath."

—**Mindy Relyea,** certified End of Life Doula and Grief Advocate

"Candid and refreshing, packed with wonderful metaphors about life and death, learned over decades of helping patients near the end of life. Everyone should read this book!"

—**Eduardo Bruera, MD,** F. T. McGraw Chair in the Treatment of Cancer, Department of Palliative, Rehabilitation, & Integrative Medicine, University of Texas MD Anderson Cancer Center

"Ana Claudia is a rare poem walking on two legs, dressed in a white lab coat, with two eyes shining on every face she encounters. If 'death is the bridge to life,' her words in *Death Is a Day Worth Living* become something equally rare: the warm and willing hand clasping yours, walking you across that rickety bridge, under a generous sun."

—**Dallas Graham,** founder and publisher of the Red Fred Project

Praise for *A morte é um dia que vale a pena viver* (*Death Is a Day Worth Living*)

"Courageously deals with a subject that continues to be taboo."

—maisMINAS, Brazil

"The big question that surrounds death is, in reality, life."

—*SAPO*

"In this book, [Dr. Ana Claudia Quinatana Arantes] proposes a new look at life."

—*Rolling Stone*, Brazil

"It is death you speak about, but it is about life, our life, that you make us think."

—DN *Life*

"A delicious reflection on death—and life."

—*Jornal do Brasil*

"Ambitious and challenging."

—Slow Medicine

"*Death Is a Day Worth Living* can change people's perception of life."

—*O Globo*

"A frank, sensitive, and inspiring account of her experience caring for the dying. *Death Is a Day Worth Living* is a lesson in courage and empathy."

—Vamos Falar Sobre o Luto

Death Is a Day Worth Living

DEATH IS A DAY WORTH LIVING

DR. ANA CLAUDIA QUINTANA ARANTES

Broadleaf Books
Minneapolis

DEATH IS A DAY WORTH LIVING

Originally published in 2016 as *A Morte E Um Dia Que Vale a Pena Viver*, Sextante, GMT Editores Ltda.

This English Language Edition Copyright © 2023 by Ana Claudia de Lima Quintana Arantes. Printed by Broadleaf Books, an imprint of 1517 Media. All rights reserved. Except for brief quotations in critical articles or reviews, no part of this book may be reproduced in any manner without prior written permission from the publisher. Email copyright@1517.media or write to Permissions, Broadleaf Books, PO Box 1209, Minneapolis, MN 55440-1209.

Cover image: Stocksy/Thais Varela
Cover design: Emily Weigle
Print ISBN: 978-1-5064-8772-4
eBook ISBN: 978-1-5064-8773-1
Printed in Canada

The wisdom of this book is dedicated to my greatest teachers:
the people I have cared for and their relatives.

CONTENTS

INTRODUCTION

> *"If you bring forth what is within you,*
> *what you bring forth will save you.*
> *If you do not bring forth what is within you,*
> *what you do not bring forth will destroy you."*
>
> Jesus, *The Gospel according to St. Thomas*

An invitation, a party. I arrive not knowing anyone except the hostess. I can see from her warm welcome that some of the guests are interested in meeting me, knowing who I am. They come over. I am shy on these occasions and find it hard to start a conversation. Moments later, the circle has widened and conversation flows. As it works with such gatherings, each person says a bit about who they are, what they do. I observe gestures and looks. I feel a curious urge growing in me to provoke the conversation beyond the usual niceties. I smile.

Finally, someone asks, "And you? What's your job?"

"I'm a doctor."

"Really? That's awesome! What's your specialty?"

Several seconds of doubt. How do I respond? I can say I'm a geriatrist, and the conversation will take the most obvious course. Three or four questions about hair and nail problems. With my experience, what do I recommend to slow down aging? Perhaps a question about a relative who seems to be getting "senile."

This time, though, I want to answer differently. I want to say what I do, and that I do it with great pleasure and find it highly rewarding. I don't want to shrink away from it. That inner decision makes me uneasy, but at the same time, brings a positive, liberating sensation.

"I care for people who are dying."

Suddenly there is a bottomless silence. It is unthinkable to talk about death at a party. Now the atmosphere is tense and, even at a distance, I pick up glances and read thoughts. I can hear the people around me breathing. Some look away, down at the floor searching for a hole to hide in. Others continue to stare at me with that "Excuse me?" expression, expecting me to change course, and quickly explain that this wasn't quite what I meant to say.

I have been wanting to do this for quite some time, but lacked the courage to face the awful silence I already imagined would come before anyone spoke. At the same time, I am not sorry. Inside myself, I offer consolation and wonder: Will people ever choose to talk about life this way? Can that day be today?

Then, in the midst of that embarrassing silence, someone plucks up courage and, hiding behind a veil of smiles, manages to get out: "Wow! That must be really difficult!"

Forced smiles, then silence again. Within two minutes, the group has broken up. One goes off to talk to a friend who has just arrived, another goes to get a drink and never comes back, a third heads for the bathroom, and another simply excuses herself and leaves.

It must have been a relief to the partygoers when I said my goodbyes and left after less than two hours at the party. I was relieved too, but at the same time, disappointed. Were people ever going be able to talk about death naturally and, in the process, change the way they think about it?

Were people ever going be able
to talk about death naturally
and, in the process, change
the way they think about it?

It's been more than fifteen years since the day I "came out" at that party. I continue to don my "I take care of people who are dying" hat and, despite all predictions about how that conversation will disperse any party, talking about death as a part of life in all sorts of settings is gaining ground.

Where do I see evidence of that? For starters, early on, many people asked me to write this book, because they knew there was a need for it. My book became a bestseller in Brazil the year it came out, and continues to be an international bestseller in its now various translated editions. But even before all of that, there were those who believed in my message, telling me many people would read this book.

WHO I AM

"I had a girlfriend who used to see everything wrong. What she saw was not a heron by the river. What she saw was a river by a heron. She undid whatever was considered normal. She said that its opposite was plainer than day. With her, things had to change how they behaved. In fact, the girl once told me that she had daily encounters with her contradictions."

Manoel de Barros

I see things differently, in ways most people do not allow themselves to, and I have taken countless opportunities to engage with people who are interested in changing their position, changing their point of view. Only a few of them manage to change, while others really need to. What unites us in the wanting to change is this: a desire to see life differently, to head down a new path, because life is short and needs to be understood as valuable, meaningful and significant—and death is an excellent reason to find a fresh way of looking at life.

This book has brought you and me together, and I hope to be able to share something of all I have learned, as a doctor, day after day in my work, and also as a human being who looks after other intensely human beings. I have to say, from the outset, that knowing about someone's death does not mean that you necessarily become part of the person's life story. Not even being present at someone's death is enough to earn you that privilege. Each one of us is present in our own life and in the lives of those we love—present not just physically, but present with our time, our actions. It is in that loving presence alone where we sense that death is not the end.

Nearly everyone thinks it's normal to shrink from the reality of death—but the truth is that death is a bridge to life.

You have to unlearn what you've long considered is "normal."

Nearly everyone thinks it's normal to shrink from the reality of death—but the truth is that death is a bridge to life.

WHY I DO WHAT I DO

"Do you want to be a doctor, my son?

That is the aspiration of a generous soul, of a spirit zealous for knowledge.

Have you really thought about what your life will be like?"

Asclepius

As I write this book, I am probably more than halfway through my life on this earth and have been practicing Medicine for more than twenty years. Many choices of profession pose their own set of questions, the field of Medicine among them. Why Medicine? Why did I choose to be a doctor? One reason many give for following this path is that there were doctors in the family, people they admired. But not for me; in my family there were none. Though there had always been disease and suffering, ever since I was very little.

My first step toward choosing this profession had to do with my grandmother, who suffered from peripheral artery disease and eventually had to undergo two amputations. She lost her legs to excruciatingly painful ulcers and gangrene. She vented her pain with agonized screams and tears. She begged God for pity and implored God to take her. In spite of all the limitations imposed on her by the disease, she focused on my education and looked after me.

On her worst days, she was visited by Dr. Aranha, a vascular surgeon. I remember him as an angelic, almost supernatural figure: a large man, gray hair carefully combed back with Gumex, a powerful fixing gel. He smelled nice and I remember him as very tall. Maybe he just looked that way to me because I was only five. And he always wore a starched white shirt and a belt of scuffed leather, the buckle gleaming. In one of his large, red hands he carried a little black bag. My eyes followed the movements of those hands and wanted to see everything that happened in my grandmother's bedroom, but whenever he came to visit, I was sent to another room.

Every so often, though, they would forget to close the door completely, leaving it ajar. Those times I would watch the whole visit through the crack. She would tell him about her pains, about her sores. She would cry and he would console her and take her hands in his. To me, it seemed those enormous hands could hold all her suffering. Then he would change her dressings and explain any new kinds of care to my mother. He would leave a prescription for her, and then on his way out he would stroke my head and smile.

"And what do you want to be when you grow up?"

"A doctor."

LIFE IS MADE OF STORIES: HERE'S WHAT I DID WITH MINE

"The moment has come to accept in full the mysterious life of those who will one day die."

Clarice Lispector

To me, Dr. Aranha was the most powerful and mysterious being on earth. After treating my grandmother, he always stayed for a visit. Over cups of coffee, tapioca powder biscuits, and orange cake, he engaged in more sociable talk, gesticulating with those enormous hands as my attentive little eyes watched. When it was time to go, he kissed me on the forehead—making me want to kiss foreheads too. In his wake, he left a trail of peace. It was amazing how much my grandmother improved just from seeing him. My grandmother, full of hope for the new prescription, would start smiling again.

Life went on with its ups and downs, but as I mentioned before, the natural course of the disease led to my grandmother's having both legs amputated. The hope that her suffering would lessen after the amputation was short-lived: the pain continued on. My grandmother had what the doctor called "phantom pain," a diagnosis terrifying to a child. Phantom pain? Couldn't it be exorcised? Sent on its evolutionary course, away? Taken from purgatory and set free to ascend and take a different form in heaven? Or couldn't we damn it to hell, where it would remain for all eternity and never plague anyone here ever again?

"What can I do while I'm still alive," I asked myself, "to combat phantom pain?" Even praying did not help heal her legs or relieve her pain.

I decided to amputate the legs, thin and fat, of all my dolls. Not one escaped the cruel fate of similarity. Rosita alone was left intact: she'd come from the factory with her legs crossed like a Buddha. To this day, I wonder if choosing to remain seated forever protects you from walking and thus losing your legs at some point in life. But Rosita did get "surgical" ballpoint markings, just to remind me that, even if I wanted to keep sitting, life would leave its marks.

So it was that, at seven years old, I was already running a ward giving care to dolls in pain. Except at my hospital, no one was in pain. In between administering medications, I would place them all in a row and teach them what I had learned at school.

My grandmother found these scenes amusing and always asked, "Changed your mind? Going to be a teacher?"

"I'm going to be both, Gran! When their pain goes away, they want to learn!"

My grandmother would laugh and tell me she wanted to be treated in my hospital—and I promised I would take care of her and she would never feel pain again. I asked if, once the pain had gone away, she was going to want classes too. She said she would.

"Will you teach me to read?"

"Of course I will, Gran!"

She smiled. My childish certainty must have delighted her.

When I was eighteen, I entered São Paulo University. At first, it was hard to believe I was studying Medicine, the entry-level courses were so bleak—Biochemistry, Biophysics, Histology, Embryology. All we saw of human life was death, in Anatomy class. I remember the first lesson all too well: in the vast hall, lots of tables covered with the body parts of dead people. Cadavers. I thought I would be scared, but they were so different and strange that I ignored my classmates' whimpers and moans of dread.

I started by searching the room for a face and found the corpse of someone who looked young. The expression was one of pure ecstasy. I mentioned it to a fellow student beside me.

"Look at his face! He must have died looking at something really beautiful."

The girl recoiled, staring at me as if I were an alien, an extraterrestrial. "You're weird," she said.

In that room, I tried to imagine all of the possible stories each face told among the study "specimens." As I did, the other students began to look at me more and more like ET and, truthfully, I felt more "alien" as the course progressed. At the end of my third year, I learned how to conduct an anamnesis (the initial interview a doctor has with a patient). I assumed the detailed guide that taught students how to talk to a sick person would lead me down safe, conventional paths.

Right away, I discovered how wrong I was. When we were assigned cases in the Internal Medicine ward, I was to meet and interview Antônio. My professor had filled me in on the key facts about the patient: male, married, alcoholic, smoker, two children, liver cirrhosis, liver cancer and hepatitis B; end-stage. At that time, the doors to the rooms had little square windows we could observe patients through without going in. I remember standing there at the window for quite a while, my heart racing in anxious anticipation of talking to a patient with such a complex history for the first time.

What I could not imagine was how that meeting would stir up a whirlwind of discoveries, fears, guilt and fathomless torment inside of me.

I entered the room with a sense of profound respect and fear. Antônio was sitting in a metal chair, the enamel cracked and peeling, looking out the window. He was a scary sight: emaciated, but with an enormous belly, like a giant four-legged spider, his skin dark and yellowed, his face creased with deep wrinkles. His body was covered in bruises, as if he had taken a rough beating. He welcomed me with a nod of the head and a polite, toothless smile. I introduced myself and asked if we could talk for a while.

He went over to the bed and, with great difficulty, labored up the steps and slowly laid down. I started the painful interview by asking about his past: When had he started to walk? To talk? What illnesses had he experienced as a child, and what was his family background like? Then I asked about the history of his present condition. His main complaint was the ache in his abdomen, just under the ribs on the right-hand side. He said his belly was so big he had a hard time breathing. At night he was very scared and the pain got worse—and, as the pain got worse, the fear grew too.

Antônio told me he was afraid to be alone, afraid of being by himself when it was time to die. He was also afraid of not waking up in the morning. His eyes brimming with tears, he said he deserved it all. He had been a really bad man all his life. His wife said that God was punishing him. He thought she might be right.

The gulf between what he was saying and what I wanted to say grew wider with every passing moment. I was beginning to realize how impossible it was to say anything at all in the presence of so much suffering. Instead, I withdrew into myself and retreated behind a wall of silence.

The time had come, I decided, to examine him, but I could not go on. I could not bring myself to touch that body. Now it was me who was afraid. I had this sense, like a waking dream, that if I touched him I might feel his pain. At the same time, I was afraid that by touching him I would cause him even more pain.

I left his room to get help.

First, I tried the nurses' station. The floor nurse barely raised her eyes from her notes when I asked if she could give António more medication to ease his pain.

"He just had Dipyrone. You have to wait for it to take effect."

"But he's still in so much pain! And it's been over an hour since they gave him the medication," I answered.

"There's nothing to be done except wait for the next dose, five hours from now," she said.

"But what about now? Is he going to be in pain all that time? What do you mean, there's nothing to be done?"

"Listen, dearie," she shot back with a touch of irony, "the day you get to be a doctor, you can give more medication. I've talked to the attending doctor and tried to persuade him to sedate the patient. António needs to die as soon as possible."

"Die? But can't he at least be in less pain until he dies?"

The nurse dropped her gaze and her attention vanished into the paperwork in front of her.

I saw there was no point insisting and went to look for the professor. I found him in the doctors' lounge, having coffee with other professors. I told him he needed to give the patient more analgesic before I could go on with the examination because he was in a lot of pain. I was reprimanded. After all, I had been told that this was a terminal patient, and there was nothing that could be done for him.

That was when I understood what it meant to die from an incurable disease in a hospital: all the world's suffering in one single person, and all the terrible voices echoing, "Nothing to be done. . . . Nothing to be done."

By the first term of my fourth year, I had seen a lot of deaths, both expected and unexpected: children with severe diseases and violent deaths, teenagers with AIDS and cancer, and many, many older people consumed by years of suffering from debilitating, chronic diseases. I saw many die alone at the door of the emergency room—and every time that happened, it strengthened my certainty that I could not go on.

Halfway through my fourth year of Medicine, I left the university.

Crises close to home hit hard: in addition to various health problems among my family members, we were facing serious financial difficulties. My situation at home gave me a good excuse to leave the university—I needed to get a job. Instead, I spent two months staying in the house, not going out at all, not knowing what to do with my life. I caught a severe case of pneumonia, but refused to go to the hospital. For the first time in my life, I wanted to die.

Once I made it through the most difficult stage, I went to work in a department store. But every day I grew increasingly anxious about my true vocation. My calling was to Medicine, but I did not know how to answer the call. Time went by and I distanced myself from what felt like a world of horrors, of abandoned lives, waiting to die in the hospital. The call echoed on in my heart, though, until I could not silence it any longer. I decided I had to keep going, even if I didn't have the talent for it. Who knows? Maybe I would get used to it after all, like other people did.

I decided to go back to school and work as a volunteer in a maternity facility in an underresourced neighborhood. There, I spent my nights massaging the backs of laboring mothers who had no option but to howl in pain. At that time, the government would not authorize anesthesia for normal deliveries, so women had no choice but to suffer. I even started to think I had finally found a way to be a doctor without having to deal with so much unnecessary suffering. The pain these women experienced would pass and the joy of meeting their babies would make those trying moments worthwhile. Like Nietzsche, I believed that people will tolerate any "how" as long as there is a "why."

A year later, I finished my fourth year without too much suffering on the part of the living patients and had fallen under the spell of something completely different, something I had never thought about before: a course in Forensic Medicine I was taking and loved. It involved attending autopsies at the medical examiner's office and at the morgue, as well as Clinical Anatomy classes, where patient cases were presented and doctors discussed diagnostic hypotheses. At the end of the class, the pathologist would come up and present the autopsy findings, which would make the cause of death clear. In my fifth year, I started to work shifts, and my first internship was in Obstetrics. As I had already been handling deliveries in the other maternity unit, I did really well. By then I was certain it really was Medicine I loved.

Throughout my time in medical school, whenever I saw someone die with great suffering (and at a hospital that is nearly always the case), I would ask what could be done. Nearly everyone would respond with "Nothing." It affected me profoundly—that "nothing" sat like a painful weight on my chest. I found myself crying often: crying with rage, frustration, and compassion.

What did they mean, "nothing"? I could not accept the other doctors' unconcern at such incompetence—not in failing to avert death, because no one lives forever, but in their abandoning patients and their families. Why? Why refuse to give more to alleviate the pain? And why sedate the patients and close them off from all communication? There was such an enormous distance between what I was learning and the questions that continued to torment me, unanswered.

People soon started to make fun of me as the doctor who couldn't stand the sight of a sick patient. Is there even such a thing? No, there is not. I hid myself away in the medical school Photography department. No one sees the tears behind the camera. No one can read the photographer's soul until they show their work. To my way of thinking, I was seeing things others missed, but it was still too early to share my perspective and say what I felt was true. I kept quiet and pressed on.

In his book *Being Mortal* North American surgeon and writer Atul Gawande writes, "I learned about a lot of things in medical school, but mortality wasn't one of them." No one at medical school talks about death, about what it is like to die. They do not discuss how to care for someone in the final stage of a severe, incurable disease. One by one, the professors ducked my questions. Some even went so far as to say that I should move into a specialty that involved little or no contact with patients. They said I was too sensitive and would be unable to care for patients without suffering as much as they themselves did, or more.

Without a doubt, going through the undergraduate coursework was the hardest time in my life. At the end of that period, I chose Geriatrics. I thought if I looked after older people, maybe I would come to regard death as something more physiological and natural. The first step in that learning process happened to be when a nurse handed me a copy of *On Death and Dying* by Elisabeth Kübbler-Ross, a Swiss psychiatrist who moved to the United States. In the book, she describes her patients' experiences as they approach the end of their lives as well as her desire to get close enough to help them in their final moments. I devoured that book in a single night, and by the next day, that pain sitting on my chest had eased. I even managed to smile as I promised myself: I'm going to learn what can be done.

I soon began doing shift work in the emergency ward, where I could think and act more independently. The work felt easier now, because I understood disease processes in a way I hadn't before. I felt calmer and saw that giving patients attention helped them improve more quickly. I enjoyed talking to them and finding out about their lives outside of the hospital, beyond their diseases. I liked to dig for stories like someone digging for treasure—and with every patient, I always find stories.

I liked to dig for stories like someone
digging for treasure—and with
every patient, I always find stories.

CARING FOR THE CAREGIVERS

"Love thy neighbor as thyself."

Jesus, the Gospel of Matthew

Throughout my work as a doctor, long before embracing my destiny publicly, I lived in a way that was consistent with my bold purpose: to care for people who are dying. I like to care for those who are most aware of their death. The suffering that hangs over this stage of human life cries out for care and I have devoted a large part of my life to studying Palliative Care. The whole focus of my professional career has been that multidimensional, comprehensive care that Medicine can offer patients coping with severe, incurable illnesses that threaten to end their lives. I take that focus even further: my life became more meaningful when I discovered that caring for yourself is just as important as caring for others.

Like most health professionals, though—especially doctors—for quite a long time I failed to give much importance to that invaluable discovery. It seems more socially acceptable to say you don't have time for lunch, don't have time to sleep, don't have time to exercise, to laugh, to cry—don't have time to live. Job dedication seems to be tied to one's social recognition—a twisted way to feel important and valuable.

Everyone around you should be convinced that the world only turns because you as a medical professional are pushing.

Three pagers, two smartphones, shifts nearly every weekend—and steeped in financial difficulties as I helped my parents and sisters stay afloat. That was how I worked, tirelessly, for five years, as an assistant to a team of oncologists.

In my last year with the group (by now I was being recognized for my study of Palliative Care, my gift for empathy, and my commitment), my supervisors appointed me to accompany many of our patients into home care. These were people in advanced stages of cancer with no hope of cure or control, who received Palliative Care at home.

My experiences with the home care teams varied from bad to very bad, in large part because the staff involved had no idea what Palliative Care was. The toll that both my schedule and this process took on me was impossible to sustain—until Marcelo came into my life, the twenty-three-year-old diagnosed with intestinal cancer. His aggressive disease showed no responsiveness to oncological treatment and, when he was discharged from the hospital, his mother insisted that I be the one to continue his care at home. She knew her son had a terminal disease and wanted to be with him at the family home, which was his wish too. I accepted, flattered.

The first visit to their home was simply about managing the pain. In a few days, the pain was under control, but that led to Marcelo constantly being drowsy. As the disease progressed to his liver, he began hallucinating and crying out in fear.

One Friday evening, with São Paulo under heavy rain, I arrived at the house to find Marcelo's abdomen forced out of shape by tumor masses. He vomited once, twice, three times. Blood and feces pooled together in his bedroom, which now smelled of death. He shouted then saw me, held out his arms toward me, and smiled. Soon after, he yelled again, his eyes reflecting his terror—the worst fear I have ever witnessed.

The nursing technician was petrified. In the living room, his mother and grandmother cowered behind mantras and incense. The smell was unbearable: blood, feces, incense, fear. Death.

I opened the emergency bag I had ordered for his final moments. All I found inside were vials of drugs for resuscitation. What I needed was morphine—for him, for me, for all of us. Something to subdue all the pain and powerlessness we felt.

I called the hospital to request the drugs, but we were told we would have to wait for them to arrive. And his mother did not want to take him back there. She promised him she would take care of everything at home.

"Help me!" he begged.

We waited nearly four hours for the morphine. The nursing technician was shaking so violently she could not even prepare the injection, so I prepared it, gave it, waited, and consoled him. He fell asleep. Peace reigned in the house at last; the mother thanked and hugged me.

That day, I didn't know who I was. I got in my car, the rain coming down like a flood, and I cried. My tears fell in torrents, but the rain drowned out my sobs. It fell everywhere.

The phone beside me rang; the nursing technician: "Dr. Ana? I think Marcelo's heart has stopped." I had to go back in to write up the death certificate. *Would I survive this?* I wondered. I looked out at the night. At the sky. The rain had stopped. Death came within the lull.

Back home, during a night of troubled sleep, reliving the scene and hearing "Help me!" I screamed as I awoke from the nightmare. I went to the bathroom and washed my face. Looking in the mirror, I saw Marcelo. I thought, *My God, I'm hallucinating. . . . Or am I still dreaming?*

I called my therapist for help; I cried, I begged, I confessed: "I can't stand any more of this! I don't want to see another patient! I don't want to be a doctor!"

After that horrific night, I took time off of work for forty-two days. No phone, no pager. Then I went back and handed in my resignation. Gradually, life returned to normal. A lot of coffee, a lot of tea, a lot of conversations, especially with Cris, my therapist at the time. I began to learn the explanation and a term for what had happened to me: compassion fatigue.

I conducted a retrospective diagnosis of myself after experiencing Marcelo's death: acute, intense, secondary post-traumatic stress. Compassion fatigue occurs with health professionals whose primary gift to someone suffering is empathy. People present with that much suffering end up absorbing pain that is not theirs.

And what was I supposed to do now? I had so many questions still unanswered—the most tormenting of all being, How do I deal with other people's pain without taking it on myself?

In therapy, I found more chasms than bridges. Time and time again, the height of all those terrifying crags and cliffs left me feeling like I had no horizon, no still point I could look to for answers. Wherever I turned, there was always a challenge, some unfinished business, leaving me asking, So what now? What was the point of it all?

March 1, 2006

A tense day. I get to the hospital before seven, and already four patients have been admitted to the floor and are waiting for me to see them. I haven't had time to talk to the doctor who did the evening round and I am late. How someone who gets out of bed exhausted manages to be late already, at seven in the morning, is a mystery to me. I need to read the patient

34

records and get an update on the past twenty-four hours. My colleague's handwriting is no help. I'm irritated. My stomach hurts. I think I should cut down on the coffee.

I go into the first room: woman, thirty-nine years old, divorced. Her teenage son is still fast asleep on the guest sofa. The woman whimpers. She has metastatic lung cancer. She is a nonsmoker. The pain is still very intense, even though she has been on a morphine pump for three days. It is difficult to establish the ideal dose, because she is very sensitive to the side effects. For an instant, I see the scene from a new point of view: as I observe the woman, all of a sudden, I become her.

This is an enormous shock. I feel my heart palpitating so much it hurts. Me, with palpitations again? Am I going arrhythmic? Must be all that coffee. The erratic heartbeats scare me. I look at the patient again and now see her as separate from me. My God, can I be hallucinating? I think I should stop taking medicine to sleep; even though it's just a simple antihistamine, it is starting to become a routine: insomnia nearly every night. In fact, I go four nights without sleeping, then on the fifth, I am worn out and fall into a deep sleep. Then I wake up at three in the morning and cannot go back to sleep. Tachycardia. There is something wrong with my heart. Must be the coffee.

"Is there any other way to save yourself, except by creating your own realities?"

Clarice Lispector

March 6, 2006

Rethinking my therapy. Nothing makes much sense. Palpitations. Again. I should take a break. I don't seem to be going anywhere, even though I can't stop for anything. I'm tired of just talking about my problems. For nearly three months now, I've been trying to meditate, but the result: nil. All my results add up to nothing. The world has been gray for some time now, but I keep moving as though on autopilot. It's four in the morning and all I do is turn things over and over in my mind. I've got a stomach ache. I fall asleep. It's so good to sleep! Nearly ten minutes, then my cell rings: "Dr. Ana? Mr. Smith has just been admitted to emergency. The family wants to know what time you are coming in to see him." I glance at the clock: it's six thirty in the morning. I'm coming, I'm coming. I'm going over the edge. Today I've got a new ache: my back throbs and it's all I can do to sit. I have to walk. Life keeps ordering me: "Get going!"

March 8, 2006

"Hi, Annie, darling! You're coming to the Women's Day event, aren't you, my love?"

Women's Day is today, but the commemoration at the São Paulo Medical Association will not be for another two days. I want so much to say, "No, dear, no way am I going." But I don't, and I say, "Yes, of course I'll be there." It will be on a weekday, a day when I'll need a clone to be able to do everything I've promised. The palpitations have increased. Even thinking about everything I'm planning to do makes my heart feel like it's beating inside my throat and mouth. My stomach boils like a volcano. My back throbs. I'm in so much physical discomfort that it distracts me from the discontent in my soul. I'm going to stop going to therapy. Too expensive and I'm up to my neck in debt. I'll go on helping the family out; can't bring myself to refuse. I never refuse anything, I'm always available to help. And I do help.

March 9, 2006

Doctor's visit. A thirty-nine-year-old woman is in agony. In the active process of dying. Her ex-husband has come to visit her. I talk to him in the hospital corridor. The suffering is nearly over. The son sits on the waiting room sofa, gazing into the abyss of the floor under his feet. His sneakers are ripped. A little pool of tears gathers beside an untied lace. The scene hurts so much inside my chest that I lose my balance. My stomach aches in sympathy. Must be the coffee I need to cut out. Must be the therapy that's too expensive. Must be my debts I can't pay off. Yes, must be the insomnia. There's something wrong with my heart.

March 10, 2006

I'm going to the Women's Day celebration at the São Paulo Medical Association. My cell phone is full of messages from people who admire me and congratulate me. Women are supposed to be flexible, but I'm doubled over. My back aches like never before.

I've promised Iraci, the woman who organizes the events, that I will go, and I can't disappoint her. I can't disappoint the whole world. I have this great plan to beat the rush hour traffic, but I leave in the middle of the city's rush hour.

I arrive somewhat late, but the event is delayed anyway. There's nowhere to sit, so I stand in a corner of the side entrance stairway. My back's going to lock up today—I can't get the thought out of my head. Then the tributes are over and my mind wanders. They begin the night's special presentation: "Gandhi, Leader and Servant."

The actor is brilliant. How can people transform themselves like that when they play a part? I find myself wondering about the roles I've been playing and how I've done badly. I'm not a good mother, nor a good wife. I've made every effort to be a good doctor, but I'm starting to doubt what I do. Talking to friends today just irritates me, because they've had all the same complaints for years. Why don't people change? Why don't I change—my life, my hair, my country, my planet? Exhausted, I feel my back pain coming on strong, but I don't move. I deserve that pain as my companion as I watch the play unfold.

A mother takes her son to Mahatma Gandhi and begs him, "Please, Mahatma, tell my son not to eat sugar."

After a pause, Gandhi tells the mother, "Bring your son back in two weeks."

Two weeks later, she returns with her son. Gandhi looks deep into the boy's eyes and says, "Do not eat sugar."

Thankful, but perplexed, the woman asks, "Why did you ask me to wait two weeks? You could have said the same thing to him before!"

Gandhi answered, "Two weeks ago, I was eating sugar."

The play ends, but I stand there, unable to clap, staring at Gandhi, my soul laid bare. It's an epiphany, definitely an epiphany. In an instant, I understand what the next great step in my career, my life, is to be.

I realize that the great answer I have been looking for is this: all my work giving comprehensive care to people as whole human beings only makes sense if, first, I am committed to caring for myself and my own life. I remember when I used to be a very religious person, and one of Jesus's most important teachings comes to mind: "Love thy neighbor as thyself." I realize that everything I am doing for my patients, for my family, for my friends, is one vast, immense, unbearably burdensome hypocrisy.

This realization fills me with a strength and a peace I never thought possible. From now on, I will make sure that my feet stay on the right path: I can take care of the suffering of others, because I am taking care of my own.

WHAT IS PALLIATIVE CARE?

In 2002, the World Health Organization established a revised definition of Palliative Care for adults, with a separate one for children.

THE WHO'S DEFINITION OF PALLIATIVE CARE FOR ADULTS

Palliative Care is an approach that improves the quality of life of patients and their families facing the problem associated with life-threatening illness, through the prevention and relief of suffering by means of early identification and impeccable assessment and treatment of pain and other problems, physical, psychosocial and spiritual.

PALLIATIVE CARE

- provides relief from pain and other distressing symptoms

- affirms life and regards dying as a normal process

- intends neither to hasten nor postpone death

- integrates the psychological and spiritual aspects of patient care

- offers a support system to help patients live as actively as possible until death

- offers a support system to help the family cope during the patient's illness and in their own bereavement

- uses a team approach to address the needs of patients and their families, including bereavement counseling, if indicated

- will enhance quality of life, and may also positively influence the course of illness

- is applicable early in the course of illness, in conjunction with other therapies that are intended to prolong life, such as chemotherapy or radiation therapy, and includes those investigations needed to better understand and manage distressing clinical complications.

THE WHO'S DEFINITION OF PALLIATIVE CARE FOR CHILDREN

Palliative Care for children represents a special, albeit closely related field to adult palliative care. The WHO's definition of Palliative Care appropriate for children and their families is as follows; the principles apply to other pediatric chronic disorders.

Palliative Care for children is the active total care of the child's body, mind and spirit, and also involves giving support to the family.

- It begins when illness is diagnosed, and continues regardless of whether or not a child receives treatment directed at the disease.

- Health providers must evaluate and alleviate a child's physical, psychological, and social distress.

- Effective Palliative Care requires a broad multidisciplinary approach that includes the family and makes use of available community resources; it can be successfully implemented even if resources are limited.

- It can be provided in tertiary care facilities, in community health centers and even in children's homes.

The distress of being made aware of your own mortality does not start with the process of dying. Though a possible diagnosis as you await test results might be your first glimpse of it, suffering accompanies the entire process from confirmed diagnosis of a severe life-threatening disease through to death. A disease, an interpretation of a set of signs and symptoms associated with laboratory and imaging tests, is something that any number of individuals can share in common; for the thousands of people with cancer, it may even lead to practically identical outcomes.

The related suffering, however, is singular, unique and totally individual.

In our day-to-day as health professionals, we see diseases repeated, but the suffering is never the same. Even though the treatment may offer relief from pain, the experience of pain hinges on specific mechanisms of expression, perception, and behavior. Each person is unique. All pain is unique. How suffering is expressed differs completely, even in identical twins who share the same DNA.

When a person is diagnosed with a severe disease, their suffering begins immediately. Although impending death may possibly hasten an encounter with the meaning of life, it also brings with it the anguish of perhaps not having enough time to experience that encounter. Palliative Care thus offers not just the possibility of suspending whatever treatments can be considered futile, but also the tangible reality of expanded care offered by a team to address the physical suffering, the advancing disease's symptoms, and the aftereffects of the aggressive treatment required to control a severe, incurable disease. As patients come to realize their own mortality, the emotional suffering involved is intense—and it is that awareness that leads them to look for meaning in their existence.

I always say that Medicine is easy—too simple, even, compared with the complexity of the field of Psychology. With a physical examination, I can evaluate nearly all of a patient's internal organs. With a few laboratory and imaging tests, I can deduce quite precisely how well their vital processes are functioning. However, no matter how much I observe a person, I cannot discover where they find peace or how much guilt runs in their veins along with the cholesterol, or how much fear they carry, or even if they are being poisoned by loneliness and neglect.

In the presence of a severe illness and the inexorable journey toward death, the family falls ill too. The difficult stages of a family member's physical disease are often framed by a context of disintegrating, or ever-stronger, bonds of affection. Depending on the place the person occupies in the family, there may be moments of great fragility for all of them, bound as they are by strong emotional ties—be they good or bad, easy or difficult—of love and tolerance, or even of hatred. The experience of the disease has consequences that affect everyone, and the patient's support network can help or hinder during this time in their lives.

There is also a spiritual dimension to the human being who falls ill. At such times, in the clear awareness of your own finiteness, that dimension gains a voice it never had before. The great risk here, though, is that the spiritual dimension, if improperly structured or if built on a cost-benefit relationship with God or with whatever is held sacred, may collapse in ruins at the realization that nothing is going to postpone the Great Encounter, the End, Death. The greatest pain often comes from the feeling of being abandoned by a God who does not submit to our wishes and simply disappears from our lives at these difficult times of such great suffering.

There is also a spiritual dimension to the human being who falls ill. At such times, in the clear awareness of your own finiteness, that dimension gains a voice it never had before.

Palliative Care can be useful at any stage of a disease, but it becomes especially valuable and necessary when the disease progresses to high levels of physical suffering and Medicine has nothing more to offer. That's when the prognosis is settled, imminent death is announced, and the doctors declare, "There is nothing more to be done." But I discovered that it is not true; no treatments may be available for the disease, but there is much more that can be done for the person who has the disease.

My quest for greater understanding about how to care for people with severe, incurable diseases, in all their dimensions, especially as they approach the end of their lives, has always involved a lot of effort and stubbornness (these days, they do not say I am stubborn; I am "determined"). Stubbornness and determination spring from the same source, but their identities are revealed only at the end of the story: if you fail, it was stubbornness; if you succeed, it was determination.

Driven by that energy, I often come up with more questions than answers. I can see the importance of my work for patients in need of Palliative Care. I cannot say whether choosing Palliative Care was a good or bad decision on my part, but I do see it as absolutely indispensable in affording patients a good quality of life in the time they have remaining.

The diagnosis of a terminal illness leaves only one certainty: unbearable suffering lies ahead. Having someone who cares about that suffering as life comes to an end is a source of great peace and comfort—both for the person who is dying and for their loved ones.

In my profession as a doctor, working with death is part of my everyday routine. I believe all doctors should be trained never to give up on their patients, but all we learn at medical school is not to give up on their diseases. When no more treatments are available for the disease, it is as if we are no longer qualified to stand by our patient. The moment the disease becomes incurable we feel a horrible sense of helplessness, powerlessness.

Doctors trained in the illusion of having power over death are condemned to feel as though they've failed when it doesn't prove true, which happens many times in their career. Unhappiness is a constant companion of the doctor who has learned only about diseases. But doctors who have learned to give "care" with the same determination and dedication they bring to achieving a "cure" are people who experience constant fulfillment.

I do not provide care to people dying in catastrophes or emergencies. I observe my patients one by one, over the day-to-day course of their diseases. As a geriatrist, I am often lucky enough to be the one who cares for them right from the start of their journey into aging, and to me that is a tremendous privilege. I accompany them over time and come to see them as unique human beings who experience their suffering in unique ways, requiring that I be ready for the changing needs of this kind of care—and be constantly prepared. My ongoing technical and scientific education, my emotional and physical well-being, and my own self-care must all be in perfect harmony. Without that balance, I cannot give my best to what I do. I have to offer the best of my technical expertise, together with the best of my human ability. I will never be able to say that I have reached the pinnacle of perfection, but I am aware of the magnitude of the commitment I have made to myself to develop that rare, attentive eye, day after day—and that is what enables me to sleep in peace every night.

Medical technical expertise, skillfully assessing clinical histories, choosing medications, and interpreting test results all take considerable effort, but with time it gets easier. The ability to look in the eyes of those in your care—and their families—and acknowledge the importance of the suffering involved in each life story must be a fully conscious act, not a robotic one. I have to keep my full attention on every gesture and take the greatest care with my words, my gaze, my attitudes, and most importantly, with my thoughts. All have to be absolutely transparent to the person close to death.

It is amazing how, as people approach death and feel the pain of their own finiteness, they all develop an accurate antenna for the truth. They become like oracles, sages. Tuned in to what really matters in this life with an incredible clarity. As they gain direct access to their very essence, they develop the ability to see the essence of the people around them. No one backs down against a terminal disease: witness that meeting, and you have to respect the courage of the person facing their own death. The true hero is not one who tries to evade an encounter with death, but rather one who acknowledges it as their most profound teacher.

Today, in the early twenty-first century, more than one million people in my country—Brazilians—die every year, most of them in great suffering. Of these, about eight hundred thousand know they are going to die from cancer and chronic, degenerative diseases. Nine out of every ten people reading these words will at some point in their lives face their own mortality in a very real way by living with a severe disease. One day we will all become part of that statistic, and what is most painful is that so will our loved ones.

In 2010, a survey by the British magazine the *Economist* evaluated the quality of death in forty countries. Brazil ranked as the third worst country in the world to die in. We were (barely) ahead of Uganda and India. Quality of death was evaluated by indices including the availability of and access to Palliative Care, related undergraduate training for health personnel, the number of palliative care beds available, and so on. When the survey was repeated in 2015 to include other countries, Brazil ranked forty-second among the eighty-three nations rated—with Uganda ahead of us. I am happy to learn of the enormous efforts made by teams in Uganda, whom I know personally, but am saddened to see how difficult my own country finds it to set goals compatible with our needs. This shows me, with painful clarity, that our society is not prepared and that our doctors, as part of this struggling society, choose to remain ignorant about the reality of their own deaths and are not prepared to support the process of dying, of bringing their patients to the natural ending of human life.

During that process, pain and other physical suffering will be there to tell us, "Hello, we are here to do everything possible for you to experience your dying." So when I talk about not avoiding pain, I mean hearing what pain is teaching us, what suffering has to tell us before we leave, what it tells us about the life we are living now.

We are, however, only able to consider the bigger questions about life if the pain stops. My role as a doctor is to treat physical distress with all the resources available to me. If shortness of breath passes, if all intense physical discomfort ceases, then there will be time and room for life to manifest itself. Often, when physical distress is relieved, other expressions of emotional and spiritual kinds of suffering appear. The family is relieved to see the patient physically comfortable, but then a growing urgency to talk about what is missing in their lives will emerge. Time for their thoughts to turn to the "unfinished business" they need to consider will come soon enough.

Physical relief, though, requires doctors who know how to provide that care, because it is not enough just to hold hands, just to suffer in solidarity, and to pray. Clear, specific interventions are needed in order to relieve physical suffering, and they involve a great deal of technical expertise in controlling symptoms. That knowledge is currently lacking in practically all of Brazil's medical schools. I worked in an exclusively palliative care unit at the Hospital das Clínicas of São Paulo University Medical School (HCFMUSP), where I treated people referred to the hospital who faced the very real prospect of dying in a short time—and that "short time" really was short. From the moment I greeted a patient and said "Welcome," it would average two weeks before I was then signing their death certificate. Some spent only a few hours under my care; others were with me for months, but the average was fifteen days—and that is very little time for a body in that state to feel comfortable enough to evaluate their own existence, often still searching for sense and meaning up until their final breath.

When you manage to control the physical symptoms, a life that was regarded as lost can begin again. The challenge facing the doctor is to get the assessment and treatment of the physical dimension right without sedating the patient. Unfortunately, in Brazil, everyone thinks that Palliative Care means sedating the patient and waiting for death to ensue. Some think "palliative" means supporting euthanasia or expediting death, but that is a serious misunderstanding. I do not offer euthanasia and no one I know with sound training in Palliative Care recommends or practices it.

I accept death as part of life, and I use all of the medical measures and the human care necessary to offer my patients health. By health, I mean well-being resulting from physical, emotional, family, social, and spiritual comfort. I believe that life lived with dignity, meaning, and value, in all its dimensions, can accept death as a meaningful part of that same well-lived life. I believe that death can come at the right time and will then be known for what it is, orthothanasia. But I am even more ambitious in my practice of Palliative Care: I aim to deliver and to assist at what is called kalothanasia, or "beautiful" death.

> I believe that life lived with dignity, meaning, and value, in all its dimensions, can accept death as a meaningful part of that same well-lived life.

As a practitioner—whether at the Hospital Israelita Albert Einstein in São Paulo, where I also work, or in the Hospice unit exclusively for Palliative Care at the HCFMUSP—I always observe the Palliative Sedation Index of the patients under my care. In my "galaxy of care," only 3 percent of patients need to be sedated. In my small world of assisting at kalothanasia, 97 percent of people die at their most comfortable, in moments more beautiful and intense than any scene on a big screen at the cinema. There is no director, no actors, no script, not a single rehearsal. People get it right the first time, because there can be no rehearsal for dying. As a result, a beautiful, moving scene unfolds that makes complete sense in that particular person's life history. People die as they have lived. If they never lived a meaningful life, then they are unlikely to have the chance to experience a meaningful death.

The process of dying can be intensely painful for most people, particularly when there is a lack of knowledge and expertise on the part of health professionals officiating at that sacred moment in human life. When the assisting health team is highly skilled in giving proper care for the patient's remaining time, even though it may be very short, there is the chance—however extraordinary—of them leaving this existence "through the front door", with the honor and glory befitting great heroes, as kings and queens of life itself.

Unfortunately, these conditions are still far from available to all Brazilians—and to many others in countries around the world. Not all doctors working with terminally ill patients know how to take care of terminally ill patients. Many claim that everyone knows how to give Palliative Care—it is just a question of common sense. The problem is that not everyone has common sense, although they all think they do! I have never yet heard of anyone going to a psychologist and saying, "I've come here for treatment, because I haven't got common sense."

Society needs to understand that Palliative Care has to be learned and that society has to help doctors and health personnel to do that learning, for it is an expertise involving high levels of complexity, performance, and, most importantly, fulfillment—professional but also human fulfillment.

"Palliative Care requires treating
and listening to the patient and
the family. It means saying 'Yes,
there is always something that
can be done,' in the most sublime
and loving way possible. It is
an advance in Medicine."

—Note of thanks left by a daughter
who attended her father's death

EMPATHY AND COMPASSION

"Let me not pray to be sheltered from dangers
but to be fearless in facing them.

Let me not beg for the stilling of my pain
but for the heart to conquer it.

Let me not look for allies in life's battlefield
but to my own strength.

Let me not in anxious fear crave to be saved
but hope for the patience to win my freedom.

Grant that I may not be a coward,
feeling Your mercy in my success alone;

But in my failure let me find the grasp of Your hand."

Rabindranath Tagore

Being there for someone who needs Palliative Care does not mean living that person's life for them. When someone is suffering and dying, the ability required of the person there with them is a gift, an aptitude, called empathy. Empathy is the skill of being able to put yourself in someone else's place. It also may be the most important skill for any health professional wanting to work in Palliative Care. It can—paradoxically—also be the greatest risk factor for that professional becoming incapable of providing that care.

Empathy has its dangers; compassion does not. Compassion goes beyond the ability to put yourself in someone else's place; it enables you to understand another person's suffering without being consumed or impaired by it. Compassion shields you from that risk. Empathy may run out, but compassion never ends.

Sometimes empathy is blind to itself and may lead you toward the other's suffering to the point of forgetting yourself. With compassion, in order to go toward the other person, you have to know who you are and what you are capable of.

Let me try to explain the risk of blind empathy. Suppose you have enough gas in your car to drive a hundred miles. If you drive a hundred, you will not make it back home. It is as simple as that. If you have the capacity to put yourself in another person's place, but cannot maintain emotional independence apart from them, then you run the risk of never making it back to yourself. You will have gone too far, without any idea of how far you were able to go.

Therefore, the first step for anyone wanting to become involved in Palliative Care is to know yourself, to know what you can handle, what you are willing and able to do. If you want to be there for someone who is suffering, and that means overstepping your own limits, then you will have to set up "stops" along the way to "refuel"—have a soft drink, a cup of tea or coffee, fill up the tank, go to the bathroom, take a bath, meet a friend, someone who understands, who is there for you—in order to be able to continue helping them.

Sometimes you have no choice. Sometimes, it is a person you love who is dying, and you overstep your own limits. Except, in order to cope with being there, you have first to look to yourself. The act of caring for someone who is dying without also taking care of yourself responsibly is, in my view, pure hypocrisy, blatant hypocrisy.

Anyone who cares for someone else without taking care of themselves ends up full of toxic waste from poor physical, emotional, and spiritual self-care—and waste is no good if you want to care properly for anyone. It is that simple. I often hear complaints like "I take care of my mother, I take care of my father, my sister, my husband, my children. I don't have time to take care of myself." That's where I say, "Then quit talking about it! Shame on you! To me, it's like relieving yourself in your trousers. You don't go around telling people, 'I pooped my pants!' It's embarrassing, irresponsible. And when you claim that someone else's life is worth more than yours, you are lying. You value their life enough to brag about yourself, so you can say, 'Just look how kind I am! I work myself to death looking after other people!'"

This doesn't just happen among ordinary people; it happens among health professionals working in this field, too, people who think they are being kind, but who do not take care of themselves. Empathy allows you to put yourself in someone else's place and feel their pain, their suffering. Compassion enables you to understand the other person's suffering and transform it. That is why you have to go beyond empathy. We all need people who can understand our pain and help us to transform our suffering into something that makes sense.

Compassion enables you to
understand the other person's
suffering and transform it.

FEAR OF DYING, FEAR OF LIVING

"I'm not afraid of death, but of dying, yes.

Death comes after me,

but it's me who's going to die,

my final act,

and I'll have to be present.

Just like a president

handing office to a successor,

I'll have to die living,

knowing I'm going."

Gilberto Gil

A lot of people say they are afraid of death, but I am astounded to see how they live: they drink too much, smoke too much, work too much, complain too much, suffer too much—and do not live enough. I like to provoke them and say how brave they are: they are afraid of death, but they rush madly to meet it.

People who say they fear death should fear it more responsibly. Perhaps you could say they should respect death. Fear will not save anyone in the end, nor will bravery, but respect for death brings balance and harmony to your choices. It does not bring physical immortality, but does permit the conscious experience of a life worth living, even though its sufferings are alleviated, sadness outweighed by happiness, time to drink in celebration, even to smoke, to work for fulfillment—but all in good measure, in moderation.

We may be tempted to think we can cheat death, but we are too ignorant for that. You do not die only on the day of your death. You die every day you live, whether or not you are aware that you are alive. But you die more quickly every day that you are deprived of that awareness.. You die before the day of your death when you are abandoned. You die after your death when you are forgotten.

TALKING ABOUT DEATH, TALKING ABOUT TIME

"We must accept our existence in the broadest possible sense; everything, even the unheard-of, must be possible in it. That, when you come down to it, is the only kind of courage that is demanded of us: courage to admit the oddest, the most unexpected, the most inexplicable things that we may encounter."

Rainer Maria Rilke

Time to talk about death, to let the thoughts about the meaning of dying flow, to allow yourself to be unsettled by difficult feelings. I will respect your silence as I write; in fact, it's necessary for the thoughts that I hope will well up inside of you. At times, I will be direct and my words may sting your eyes. You may even want to close this book, but I know you will be back, and we will pick up where we left off or go back a chapter or a page or two before catching up again.

We are all going to die one day. But while we live, we prepare for the opportunities that life may offer. We dream about our future and we go out and reach for it, dreams such as having a career, a family, a love or loves, children, a home of your own, to travel, to share our lives with someone.

Only when we're uncertain do we seek guidance. Who can guarantee we are going to be successful in our career? Who can say we are going to find the love of our life? Who can say whether or not we are going to have children? Who can guarantee those things? No one can guarantee any of those possibilities, but one guarantee we have is death. It doesn't matter how many years you live, how many diplomas you hold, or the size of the family you have created. With or without love, with or without children, with or without money, death, the end of it all, will come. And why is it we don't prepare for it? Why don't we talk openly about this, our one and only certainty?

> Time to talk about death, to let the thoughts about the meaning of dying flow, to allow yourself to be unsettled by difficult feelings. I will respect your silence.

The anxieties, prejudices, and fragility that conversation reveals are greater than our wish to free ourselves of those fears. There are times in our lives when words just do not come, times when you search the deepest parts of yourself for answers, meanings, truth. The time to die is one of those moments.

In *Letters to a Young Poet*, Rilke offers what to me is the most sublime explanation of the experience of the end of life. For both the protagonists of our own stories and the onlookers, death is a place where words cannot reach. The moments I have experienced assisting patients at the edge of life could never be translated into words. The best words for the experience of death are unsayable.

In human life, maybe only being born is as intense an experience as the process of dying—and that may be the very reason we're so afraid of it. Even more disturbing is the fact that we are all going to go through it and may also have the opportunity to accompany someone we love in the process.

It's important to speak about death, but also about time. And the two conversations are intertwined. As the poet Lenine wrote,

> Is it time that you need in order to see?
> Do we have that time to lose?
> And who wants to know?
> Life is so rare, so rare. . . .

When we experience time, what determines its meaning is how it was experienced. Independently of what happens, time imparts meaning to the experience. Dying slowly means there will be more time to think about death, and that is what so many people fear. As much as people want the longest possible life, they do not want more time to think about death.

Let us suppose you are willing to embark on that journey, though. You may want to consider this: What would your time be like if you were in a hospital bed, waiting for someone to enter the room? What would it be like waiting for the moment when they come to change your diaper? What would it be like waiting for your bath, your pain medicine? I think if doctors had any idea how much their brief presence is awaited, they might pay more attention to what they do and say when they are with patients and their loved ones.

In the process of dying, you distance yourself from that period of time when you were alive—that is, aware and able to decide what to do with your time. The realization that you are dying brings with it an awareness that nothing you have will remain with you. Your time here will not return, because you cannot save time. We spend time on silly things, on unnecessary suffering. Most of us squander entire life-times. And you cannot hang on to it. We cling to everything—to people, clothes, money, the car, material goods we buy and take home. But you cannot cling to time. As far as time is concerned, the only thing you can keep to yourself is not about time but the experience lived within time as it enables you to build that up constantly.

What will you do with the time that is passing? What are you doing now with your time as it passes? To me, thinking about this is the master switch that "turns on" sensible, clear-headed decisions. What do I do with my time? I once went to a job interview at a hospital. The inter-viewers asked about my curriculum, my experience. Then they told me to feel comfortable to ask questions of my own. "Why do you think I would want to work here?" I wanted to know. The interviewer stam-mered. So I asked a more personal question: "And why do you work here? Why do you invest eight hours of your day here? Why do you spend a third of your life here?"

I heard that, a few weeks after my interview, he resigned. Perhaps my questions revealed the poor use he was making of his time. When you realize you are giving up your time, killing it, then the choice of what to do with it is that much more urgent. Change has to come right away.

We often fail to fully experience time as we move through it—it's as though time goes by unnoticed. Yet you can sometimes experience a moment measured by the clock as five minutes that is so incredible, so special, that in your memory it feels eternal. Time that changes you does not depend on duration. The experience of dying has enormous poten-tial for changing you in a very short space of time.

The first psychologist who worked with me at the Hospice thought therapy sessions should be private appointments, to be experienced within a therapeutic space totally different from the hospital environment. The palliative care setting can be a far remove from that ideal, though. A psychology session conducted in a room shared with another patient, or with a relative, is quite a different experience: there are constant interruptions by nursing staff, the cleaning person, the laundry service. And therapy can get suspended because the patient is in pain or needs a bedding or diaper change. For any professional, talking about sensitive aspects of a person's life surrounded by strong smells and fears is not a comfortable experience. The psychologist was concerned this would interfere with the patient's process of understanding, their responses, the course of the person's coming to terms with death.

"Don't worry," I said to her, "death is an incredible laboratory where there's a nuclear accelerator that makes it all work." You talk to a patient in the morning, and by the afternoon he has done all that is necessary to understand the whole thing. He has asked for forgiveness, has forgiven, has settled this, that, and the other, and now everything is settled. In a little while, he will be able to try to resolve other unfinished business.

Often, in a normal assisted therapeutic process, it will take a person ten years to understand simple things about themselves. When it is time to die, though, the individual's ability to understand and decide how to use their time seems to speeds up. The person they thought they were, or even who the family thought they were, can all change completely at the end.

The last impression lasts longest. How someone behaves in loss determines the impression they will leave. If you are unhappy in your job and start to act as though you want to be fired, people around you will be left with a perception of what not to do in that profession. When you are ending a relationship, starting to be unfaithful, and then making a list of complaints to justify ending the affair, that is the poisonous impression your partner is left with.

When you fall ill, your perception of time is very different than when you are in good health. Waiting times seem to take forever. It is very difficult to wait: it is the opposite of being active. You cannot do things, so it is as if you are not actively living. "Can't I do anything now? Is there nothing I can do?" we ask. There is nothing Medicine can do, so you wait for death—and the hardest problem is not death itself, but the waiting for it.

The French psychiatrist Eugène Minkowski (1885–1972), who studied the notion of "lived time," describes three "dualities" of perspectives on time very well.

The first duality of perspective involves expectation and activity. Being in expectation of something means not doing anything, because the result does not depend on you. Expectation involves a painful perception of time.

The second duality has to do with the relationship between desire and hope. Desire involves seeking something you do not have. Hope is expectation modified by optimism. Expectation always relates to something that is to happen in the future, but hope can be in any timeframe. We can hope for a positive outcome of something that has already happened. One practical example is waiting for the result of a biopsy, waiting for the result of a procedure that has already been performed, and hoping that it is not cancer. At such moments, hope alleviates the pain.

The third duality of lived time—and the one that I find most fascinating—is prayer and ethics. Minkowski describes prayer as the relationship with something you find within yourself, where you communicate with something greater than yourself: something or someone sacred, a divinity, a god. This internal space for communicating with something greater brings into you something even more powerful. It's that moment when you have done everything in your power, and then you decide to connect with something more powerful inside you, to outdo yourself and pray—and prayer always allows you to see a better future.

It's that moment when you have done everything in your power, and then you decide to connect with something more powerful inside you, to outdo yourself and pray—and prayer always allows you to see a better future.

To Minkowski, prayer differs from meditation, which focuses us on the present, and also from orison, formal traditional and often spoken prayers (invocation, exhortation, benediction) that can relate to the past. He then speaks of the duality of prayer connected to ethical action. In prayer, you hope something greater will save you, solve the problem. In ethical action, you connect with that force, with that power that exists within you, and it leads you to do something for another that is beyond your will. That is the moment when human becomes divine.

What does that moment look like in our world? To me, one clear example of ethical action is when I hear a mother saying, "You can go," to her dying child. At first, she may have prayed for a cure, but then she connects with that force and manages to understand that the best outcome is not the one she wishes would happen. The mother in our example considers the moment and understands that the best thing for her child may be exactly what will cause her so much pain if she accepts it—but she accepts it and sets the child free, out of love.

When you connect with this greater, more sacred force within you, you are able to do good for others, genuinely for their good, because it is something that needs doing, not because it is what you want. In fact, it is something that happens independently of your wishes. When you let good happen, it flows, and time is lived as if with all the meaning of love in the world. The moment you connect with the other person and say, from the deepest part of your being, from your essence, "Let whatever is best happen," that is powerful. The best happens—and it happens quickly.

The experience of time that we can see, counted by the clock, and the experience of time that stands still generally happen when our time is meaningless. One experimental model for the absence of time is the subway. People on the underground train are never there; they are just leaving one place to get to another. In that whole crowd of people, who is present? When you ride the subway underneath the city, you think, How long before I get to my station? To many people, life is like riding the subway blindfolded: they enter a place they don't quite know the location of, they don't know where they are getting off, and they are not present for the in between! They are just riding the train. Then the door opens and someone calls, "Ana Cláudia, time to get off!" You think, What, already?

When someone close to you dies, you begin to think about your own turn, when you'll get off the train. You wonder about your own death: How many stations to go until I reach the one that is my turn?

I work with people who are seriously ill, people who, when they come to me, have exhausted any possibility of curing or controlling their disease. I have a clear idea of how important time is in their lives. These people know they have very little time.

Unfortunately, our culture meets them from a place of inadequacy—lacking in maturity, integrity, reality. Time runs out, but what most people fail to realize is that, when you look at the clock, time and time again, waiting for the day to end, in fact you are urging time to go faster, and your death to arrive more quickly. Time, though, passes in its own time, indifferent to anyone's wanting it to speed up or slow down.

What separates birth from death? Time. Life is what you do in that time, your experience. When you spend your life waiting for the day to end, for the weekend, for holidays, for retirement to come, then you are eager for your death to come more quickly. We say that life begins after work, but we have forgotten that the "live now" option is not a button you can turn on and off to suit the moment or the pleasure of living. With or without the enjoyment of it, we are alive 100 percent of the time. Time goes by at a steady pace. Life happens every day, and people rarely even take notice of it.

When you connect with this greater, more sacred force within you, you are able to do good for others, genuinely for their good, because it is something that needs doing, not because it is what you want. In fact, it is something that happens independently of your wishes. When you let good happen, it flows, and time is lived as if with all the meaning of love in the world.

HOW TO HELP SOMEONE DIE

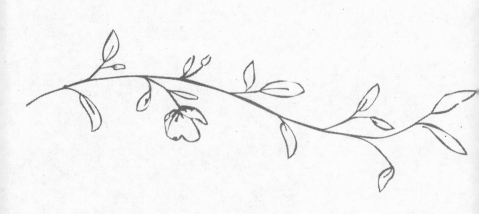

"The best thing about death, its clumsy spell, is it happens because of life."

Adélia Prado

Someone is dying before your eyes. You may feel like a bystander and that worries you. You think, *What am I going to do now?* This person is dying and what do I do for them? What can I do for them? What should I do for them? What do I want to do for them? And while you are asking yourself all these questions, time passes, life passes, and the person before your eyes passes.

Now, come with me. I see a river flowing by. I cross, wet my feet. I feel the water, cold or warm. I see the bottom or I do not, but I can feel the sand under my feet when I decide to enter, and I take my first steps. What am I doing here at the riverside? While I consider that, I find myself beside a stream of life that flows away like a river seeking the sea. I contemplate it—and the only thing I am sure of is that there is no real explanation for why people die. Many will disagree, because everyone has their theories and certainties. But, to this day, no individual, artistic, spiritual, or scientific theory or certainty has managed to tell us what life is, much less why it ends.

So I don't waste time asking that question, because it belongs in the same category as "Why does fire burn?" or "Why is water wet?" and "What does that mean?" While you are wasting time accepting illusions about what life is, you fail to get to its essence. You are missing the truth about being born and living, and you spend your life missing the truth about what it is to die.

People all die, but not all will one day learn why they lived.

People all die, but not all will one day learn why they lived. I do not know why children die. There is no explanation for that, but they do. I do not know why young people die, either, but they do too. Old people die, and although it is more or less obvious that when we get old we may die, it is not always easy accepting the reality of that fate. It is not unusual to encounter people who do not accept their loved ones' dying, even if their loved ones are very old. Whether old or young, however, successful or struggling to make ends meet, black, brown, or white, fiery lawyers, volunteers, or corrupt politicians, death will come knocking at their door. It may come with disease and suffering, whether you are ready or not. Accepting that you need to prepare for death will not help you avoid that encounter, but it can help you avoid the accompanying anxiety and turn it into a kind of respect.

Even within the complex process of caring for a human being in all their dimensions, I do not know why people die and I never will. But I do know that there is a good reason for my being there, by the bedside, by the riverside. In the presence of a person who is dying, I know that there are a lot of important things I have to do at that sacred moment of life.

What is my role in that meeting? I am there because I have to be. In my work, my purpose is to answer one single question: What can I do to make that situation the least painful, the least difficult possible? What do I have to learn in order to be there for that person and to make their suffering less than if I were not present? If people do look at death honestly enough to ask it what is most important in life, they won't find the answer.

The problem is that we live alongside people who think they are eternal. Under that illusion, they live irresponsibly, with no commitment to goodness, beauty, or truth, separated from their very essence. People who avoid talking or thinking about death are like children playing hide-and-seek in a room with no furniture: they put their hands over their eyes and think no one can see them.

Naively, they think, *If I don't look at death, it won't see me. If I don't think about death, it doesn't exist.* And people bring that same crazy logic to life itself. They think that if they do not examine their crappy emotional relationships, their crappy jobs, the crappy life they preserved at all cost, it will be as if crap did not exist. But crap will make itself known. It stinks, causes discomfort, carries disease.

They may think that, if they do not look at the dead god they cultivate in their doctrines, then that god will be well-behaved forever. They do not want to know the truth about a dead god and doctrine that is not open to the miracle of the sacred encounter. Such people live half-dead to friendship, to encounters with their peers; such people are dead within the family and dead, too, in their relation with what is sacred in their lives.

Living as if they were dead means they never really manage to live. They exist, but do not live. Many of them of surround you. I call them existential zombies. On social media, when they spread violence and prejudice, vainly insisting on staying unhappy inside and foolishly happy outside, these people increasingly cultivate their own deaths without realizing it. All of them are like strangely grown-up, sickly children, naked, with their hands over their eyes, believing they are invisible. Without knowing it, they are exposing their worst to everyone. They are absent from their own existences, which is perhaps the greatest cause for regret such people experience at the end of life.

One absence that is impossible to explain is the absence of people from their own lives. Staying connected with yourself, with others, with nature, with the world around you, and with what each of us considers sacred, requires, above all, a state of presence. There is no way to talk about death with people who are not alive in their lives.

I am not talking here about conversations with the dead; I am talking about those who are living dead, people unable to think the least bit courageously about death—existential zombies who have already buried themselves in all aspects of their humanity and wander aimlessly. All that's left is for them to die physically.

It's important here to talk about the dimensions of the process of dying. In the health field, the biological body is studied a lot. However, our biology is simply how we experience what it is to be human. And being human is not just having a working heart and lungs; it is not just the ability to keep your organs functioning enough to feel well. As humans, we endeavor to live in comfortable conditions of temperature and pressure: what scientists like to call NTP. But why do we seek normal conditions of temperature and pressure? Why do we want to have fully-working organs and body functions? So that we can have the experience of being human.

Human beings are the only species on Earth defined by a verb. Cows are cows, oxen are oxen, butterflies are butterflies, but only you are a human being. We are born as conscious, thinking, mammalian animals, but we become human only to the extent that we learn to be human. However, most of the animals of our species still do not know what that means. Only when I intentionally considered the implications of that did I finally understand what the term *humanizing* means. Until then, it seemed meaningless to talk about "humanizing" humans. But now, I see clearly that most of the conscious, thinking animals of our species behave instinctively and cruelly; they do not reflect on their thoughts, feelings, and attitudes in any depth. So the idea of humanizing people began to make sense to me. You are a "being" and completeness as a human "being" only comes about when you know how that "being" process ends. We all plan, learn, and satisfy ourselves in order to be human until the day death comes along.

And it is only through
awareness of death that we
hasten to build the being
that we ought to be.

There comes a time when we begin to take the trouble to have annual checkups, lose belly flab, look after the well-being of our children's lives. Thinking about death makes us think we have to do something about it. That's another costly mistake we often make: we start to distance ourselves from "being" by "doing." That's when we believe a good life is one full of material things that have come to us as the result of our doing things to make that "good life" happen.

But when the time of disease arrives, that's when we cannot do any more. And when we stop doing, we think that not doing is dying, but it isn't, not yet. The idea of "being" human is simply this: to exist and to make a difference wherever we are, by being whoever we are. People who have absented themselves from their own lives, when it is time to die, will be no more than "absences." Many people are like that in life, an almost constant absence—even when they are physically present, they feel that time is empty.

The idea of "being" human is simply this: to exist and to make a difference wherever we are, by being whoever we are.

Picking up again, to look at the dimensions of death: in order to help someone who is dying, you have to understand what is happening to them. The biological dimension is just a necessary condition for the other conditions to find expression. Children or elderly, whatever our color, race, creed or persuasion, we are all complex beings. We are beings who imagine the possibility of perfecting our physical dimension, because we are here, at this time and place. We also have an emotional dimension, which is the most universal of all; universal in the sense of size and complexity, though not the same for everyone. There is also a family dimension, the social dimension.

A majority of the articles and other writing on the dimensions of suffering enumerate four: physical, emotional, social, and spiritual. As I have worked in this field for quite some time now, I have taken the liberty to separate the social dimension from the family dimension. There is a complexity to the dynamics of family that is independent of the society you live in. Each family is its own microcosm, which may function well or poorly.

Politicians, however arrogant, can say or write what they like about the concept of family, but the only thing that can really define that group is the ties of love that bind its members. Not even blood ties are as strong as the comprehensive emotional bonds that connect a family. There can be families considered morally or ethically bad, but which nonetheless are functional. Each member performs a function in the family dynamics. Someone is the scapegoat, someone is the bore, someone is the phony, someone takes care of everyone else, someone is considered the (financial or existential) provider, and so on. Each one occupies a place within the family, a valuable place, essential for the family to function well; all are in balance with one other and seek to harmonize within this "mobile" design—which is why I consider the family dimension completely different from the social dimension.

The spiritual dimension can be the most intense area of suffering in the final moments of human life. An understanding of the process of dying makes life a lot easier for whoever is providing care. When you know what is going on with the various dimensions, you are in a position to conduct that process naturally, and understand death naturally too.

GIVING OURSELVES
AND OTHERS PERMISSION
TO DIE NATURALLY

"Death will be my greatest individual achievement."

Clarice Lispector

How do we define a natural death in a world where scientists and medical practitioners are talking about stem cells?

We are living in unprecedented times in Medicine; a great deal can be done to prolong human life. Nonetheless, despite all of the technological breakthroughs, we will die. A natural death presupposes the existence of a disease that runs its natural course, regardless of even the most cutting edge treatments that may be offered. A natural death is one that occurs as a result of a severe, incurable disease, which worsens and has exhausted the treatment options that Medicine has to offer. Nothing will prevent death from coming to the person with this kind of a disease; it's the inevitable end to such a situation. And it is to that person, that patient, that I offer Palliative Care.

Palliative Care, as I have practiced it for the past twenty years, is the process of caring for people who are on their last lap. Sometimes, that lap is not the last as it relates to time, but the last actually lived. Where there is a terminal diagnosis, it can last for years. Terminal does not mean "next week." In that sense, terminal is not a time period, but rather a clinical condition resulting from a severe, incurable disease that has no chance of being controlled, where the field of Medicine shrugs its shoulders. It may be experienced for hours, days, weeks, months, or even years. If the disease progresses gradually, it can take years; if it moves quickly, the person may be gone in a week or a few days.

When I began to research the process of dying related to the biological dimension, traditional medicine gave me no answers to the questions that trouble me. Technically speaking, the process that is active when death is imminent is described in terms of organ failure or even septicemia (sepsis). That is why most people who are dying are taken to a hospital and transferred to an intensive care unit—as doctors have not yet learned the difference between having a heart attack and dying. But in fact, dying is a process that can never be stopped, even if you do everything that Medicine has to offer. Once an active process of dying has started, nothing can stop its natural course.

What, then, is involved in the active process of dying? Only in Eastern Medicine have I found the answers to that question. Between my study of numerous books related to the eastern tradition and my own careful observation of the hundreds of people I have assisted in Palliative Care, I now feel more peace about how I am able to guide the family and all of those involved when a person is dying.

So what does happen when we die?

THE ACTIVE PROCESS OF DYING

"The water in a vessel is sparkling;
the water in the sea is dark.
The small truth has words which are clear;
the great truth has great silence."

Rabindranath Tagore

Eastern wisdom tells us there are four elements of nature: earth, water, fire, and air. These are also what we are made of; we, too, take form in the elements of nature. And when we die, the elements that make up our bodies will disperse.

If you think about it in terms of earth breaking apart, it is fairly evident that this breaking is about our concrete, physical being in the flesh. "Broken apart" as a disease progresses, it will advance more or less rapidly, depending on how aggressive the disease is. As it does, the body will begin to disintegrate.

The dissolution will then involve water. Biologically speaking, as people die, they tend to dehydrate and to urinate less. Production of body fluids, secretions, and enzymes in the digestive tract and bronchial tubes diminishes; the mucous membrane begins to dry. Modern Medicine understands that people die much more comfortably if they are slightly dehydrated. It is common for patients admitted to an ICU at this stage of physical deterioration to experience almost unbearable levels of discomfort. This often occurs because the doctors, ignorant about the active process of dying, flood them with liquids, resulting in large quantities of catarrh and swollen, painful skin. The kidneys will stop functioning, because this is a time for the body not to produce urine. The kidneys respect the process of the dissolution of water, even when doctors do not. That situation makes a natural death almost impossible.

Imagine a dying body struggling against that plethora of interventions that merely get in the way, because these interventions can in no way prevent death. Patients experiencing what is called "the water dispersal stage" tend to display one specific behavior: they become more introspective. They look inside themselves and into their own lives. The moment of truth has come, time to look back honestly at the path they have traveled.

At such times, some rush to prescribe an antidepressant. We know that, in today's society, you cannot just get quiet and thoughtful without someone quickly demanding: "What's happening to you? Don't be gloomy! You have to fight back! Have faith!" It seems you are not allowed to reflect on the deeper meaning of all that is happening and contemplate what your life is really about.

But, regardless of society's impositions and administering antidepressants, the water dissolution process is going to happen to us all. At a time like this, if a patient is given an antidepressant without any real indication, they will not suffer when revisiting the course of their life and choices, but neither will they manage to be happy and fulfilled with the quality of life remaining. When a patient is improperly medicated, they experience feelings and emotional stimuli as if wrapped in cellophane: there's an absence of feeling for anything at all. What results is a void. That patient will not feel cold, hot, emotion, anything at all.

Suppose, though, that the patient has not been given antidepressants and starts to get sad. The family might ask, "Are you sad? Why aren't you responsive?" They are reacting, internally. They are probing deeply as never before, searching themselves within their own essence. Because at that moment, when they are digging deep into their own essence, the dissolution of fire begins—and it is from that delving deep within themselves that patients emerge complete!

In the dissolution of fire, every single cell becomes aware that time is running out, but that there is still time to live. There is always time to take control of your own life, but it is the dissolution of fire that makes room for this awareness to manifest most fully.

You are heading for the end, but now the path becomes more beautiful and full of life. You may think that, as each of your cells recognizes the end is near, a chaos of despair would set in, a state of cell panic and total collapse. But no, that is not what happens. If you were continually connected to your cellular consciousness in this way, you would always live in harmony and balance. When every cell realizes that its time here is coming to an end, it will make every effort, one last time, to perform at its best. Your liver cells will become exemplary hepatocytes; your lung cells become incredibly skillful in gas exchange; your brain cells will come awake and all those unused neurons will rouse themselves in curiosity, survey the scene and say, "Let's see what's going on." Suddenly, your whole body is functioning properly.

You are heading for the end, but
now the path becomes more
beautiful and full of life.

So what happens to the person?

The person functions properly too. This is famously known as the pre-death surge, the rally before dying, the beautiful power of the final flicker of the candle. Dissolution of fire offers that dying person the opportunity to see what their human being came into this world for—and the person will have the chance to show the world that what brought them to this point was love.

In the dissolution of fire, what I see in nearly all of the people I have cared for in their final moments is the recognition that they came here to love and be loved. It does not matter how much baggage the person is carrying around inside; in the final flicker of their flame, that dead weight will be transformed into love. No matter who they are, they will have the chance to demonstrate that the world is good—and made better simply because they existed. If you meet the most detestable creature on the face of the Earth, full of bile, spite, and cruelty, look at them and offer a hope-filled smile; they will have a miraculous chance to be somebody better when their time comes to die.

Even people who have no advance warning of their death, those who died in accidents or from some fast-moving disease, nearly always show changes in their behavior shortly before death. A number of answers become clear at that moment of dissolution of fire and the person has—and gives themselves—permission to love, to be loved, to forgive, to ask forgiveness, to say thank you and, if they are aware of what is happening, to say goodbye. There is no set time for this, because each person takes their own time as long as I, their doctor, identify this stage and allow it to unfold naturally, along with the whole process, and I prevent unnecessary interventions.

This complex process of improving, of experiencing loving to the fullest, the expression of the person as they are in their essence, demonstrating what they came to this life for—it's a time of extreme heightened awareness within the active process of dying.

Once this dissolution of fire, the true encounter with their essence, is complete, the person will discover that something sacred lies in the depths within them. In that deepest, most sacred place lies the breath of life. The breath of life corresponds to the element air, on loan to you from God (or from the Universe) for you to fulfill your mission on Earth—and, as soon as that mission ends, you have to return it from where it was borrowed. That is when the dissolution of air begins.

This is the stage known as death throes—or literally translated *agony*—the process that most people will call "dying," because death is only fully understood to be imminent during the dissolution of air. Until then, the body is ailing; you resort to Medicine, look for treatment, do chemotherapy, have operations, take experimental drugs, sell your soul, receive the healing touch, do it all.

As water dissolves, sadness may ensue; it may or may not be mitigated by antidepressants, but it happens. The person then enters the rallying stage, a time experienced as their seeming to be fully alive. But this stage is the one followed by the agonal phase: time to return the breath of life, which will leave by the same path by which it entered—the stage of respiratory distress, when breathing is troubled, rapid or slow, then a pause followed by a deep breath. As you accompany a patient through the previous dissolutions, you are able to stay attuned to the person who is dying. Not so when air dissolves; this is different. When you want to tune in to someone, you unconsciously start to accompany their breathing. If the person is anxious, you can tune in to them so as to calm them down, or else their breathing may "contaminate" you with their anxiety. At the time of someone's death, however, it is impossible, absolutely impossible, to accompany their breathing. There is no way to tune in, unless you too are dying. You can attune to other people's emotions and even alter them, but that magic will not work in the process of death: it has started and it will end, in the ICU, in the ward, or at home; death has no preferred setting.

The most intimate experience you can have of another human being is to accompany them when it's their time. Nothing is more intimate than sharing in someone's active process of dying—not sex, nor a kiss, nor sharing secrets. At that moment, you will ask yourself what it means to be there for someone who is dying; and the person dying will search for meaning in being there; both of you will question your priorities, your burdens, fears, guilt, your truths, your illusions—all are exposed, laid bare, truly naked.

The person who is dying is naked, stripped of all physical, emotional, social, family, and spiritual disguises and, in their nakedness, can see you in the very same way. People who are dying develop a singular ability to see. Being there for someone who is dying is to stand naked too.

That is why work like mine is important. Family might ask, "How long does this last stage take?" No one knows. This "not knowing" about time frame enables you to live in the present. It offers you the opportunity to experience fullness. When you feel fulfilled, it is because your thoughts, actions, feelings, and body are all together, in the same place at the same time. Being there for someone who is approaching death can be a moment of fullness, wholeness in your life, something that happens quickly and fleetingly. Death, yours or someone else's, can be a rare and unique experience of being truly present to life.

CAN THE TRUTH KILL?

"What is good is that truth comes to us as a secret meaning of things. In our confusion, we end up divining perfection."

Clarice Lispector

It is said that telling the truth to a patient with a severe disease can kill them before their time. That is one of the biggest lies I have ever heard, and I hear it all the time. I am often faced with dilemmas by families who beg me not to tell my patients the truth about their disease, because they blindly believe that the truth will make them depressed and die before their time. They behave like children who won't open the cupboard for fear of some imaginary monster, while failing to notice the house is collapsing around them—the cupboard along with it.

What kills is the disease, not the truth about the disease. Of course, there will be sadness when learning that they are ill, seriously ill, but that sadness is the only connection they have to what's true about their life, without any illusions or false promises of a cure. What kills hope is not the discovery that you are mortal, but the feeling of being abandoned. The word that kills is the word mistakenly spoken. One of the greatest challenges I face daily is finding a way to convince families that the person who is ill has the right to know about their state of health.

When I'm teaching, I'll sometimes ask the class whether, if they had a serious disease, they would like to know the truth. Most raise their hands to indicate yes. When they do, I then caution them: "Talk to your children, your friends, your family about your request—because when you find yourself in the throes of such an illness, your children, your friends, your parents and nearly all those around you will consider you incapable of going through what you will have to live through."

All of the people who love you and think they can protect you from suffering will demand the doctors share in that unspoken belief, and, even when you are really suffering, they will tell you there is nothing wrong with you, that your health is fine and that what you feel is incorrect, not happening with your body, and it's nothing serious.

But the body does not lie. The body tells you, sometimes in a whisper, sometimes in a shout, "Something is wrong, something really bad is happening." So you think: How is it possible there's nothing wrong with me? When you come to a moment like that and the people around you have not been prepared to be there with you, that is a recipe for big trouble. When they lie, families think they are sparing their loved ones, not knowing that their loved ones also lie, to spare them.

It's common for patients to talk to me openly and clearly about their mortality. We talk about very sensitive aspects of the course of their diseases, and we even talk about their wishes for the funeral. But when these same patients talk to their families, especially the ones less prepared for their death, they make everything a fantasy: they talk about travel plans, dinners, and parties in the years to come. They seem to deny the reality of the disease, but what they are really denying is that the disease and dying can actually be talked about, because patients doubt that their loved ones will be able to cope.

When I give patients the chance to know the severity of their condition, the truth gives them the opportunity to take conscious advantage of the time they have left, to take control of their lives, of their story. By sparing someone the truth, you are not necessarily protecting them or helping them. You will not be able to save them from their own death. You will not be able to spare them from those difficult moments when they will have to be alone with themselves. When, as death approaches, you "spare" that person from grasping the urgency, the importance of the time remaining to be alive, you won't stop the dying process. You will, however, be depriving them of the chance to live.

By sparing someone the truth, you are not necessarily protecting them or helping them.

CONTEMPLATING DEATH

"To die is to just not be seen anymore. Dying is a bend in the road."

Fernando Pessoa

One of the best metaphors I have ever heard for contemplating death is to think that, in the course of your life, you will one day come up against a great wall. William Breitbart, a doctor and psychiatrist who worked with his patients on coming to terms with the meaning of life, introduced this metaphor during a lecture at a conference of experts in my field. He said you can gain a more subjective perspective on death by imagining yourself there, in front of the wall. Until that point, you walk along the path of life, sometimes sad, sometimes happy; sometimes life is dark and you do not know which way to go, but you always know you are heading somewhere. Sometimes you stop in the middle of the path and sit down, thinking: I'm rather tired, I need to rest. When you stop, you look back on what you have done so far and ahead to what you are going to do. Then, if you like, you get up and go on. The path lies ahead.

But when you are near death, you come to a wall. A great friend of mine, Leonardo Consolim, once said that he imagines the wall to be very high and long, like the Great Wall of China. I liked that image; it is what I relate to when I think about my own death. There is no getting around it, nor over it, and when you come to this wall and become aware of your own death, the only thing to do is look back. So, as you are present at someone else's death, remember this clearly: that person is looking for the path they've walked and trying to understand what they did to get to where they are—and whether the journey was worth it.

What guides your way and leads you to make good choices is the certainty that, whatever your choices, the wall is waiting. The path does not matter; they all lead to the same place. So in that sense the wall is the great equalizer. To the wall, it makes no difference if we are good people or not; we are all going to die. It makes no difference if you are honest or not; you are going to die. It makes no difference if you have loved or not, or if you have been loved. If you forgave or not. It makes not the slightest difference to the final outcome. It does not matter whether God exists or not. Religious people may dispute that last sentence hotly, but in fact, the final hour belongs to whoever is dying, and to them alone. Depending on what your relationship is with your God, this may be the worst moment of your existence or the best. If God does exist, that does not keep you from meeting the wall in the end. And if God does not exist, in the end, you also die. The discussion may center on what happens after you die, but there we will have already passed through what we dread the most.

What will happen, invariably, is that at the end of any story, any path, any choice, you are going to die—regardless of what you believe exists or not. The only thing in life to which there is no exit, no option, is death. Every other part of life has options: you can do it or not, you can want to or not—but dying or not dying is not a choice we face.

What does make the difference in the paths you choose during the course of your life is the peace you do or do not feel at this final encounter. If throughout your life your choices were someone else's, peace probably will not be present at the encounter with death.

The best thing that I can do for someone at the hour of their death is to be present. Present, there for that person, beside them, because of them, for them, in a multidimensional state of presence that only the path of compassion reveals. If I feel another person's pain, then I cannot be present, because it will be my pain. If I feel the pain, then I am in me and not in the other person. When I have compassion for the other's pain, I respect that pain, but I know that it does not belong to me. I can be present to the extent of providing support, bringing comfort. If I have compassion, I can offer or go find help. But if I feel their pain, I am paralyzed; I cannot bear to be present for this suffering and have to help myself. It is distressing to see someone else in pain, especially when you do not have a doctor with you who understands the importance of providing appropriate care. The doctors may not have the expertise, or may not want to use it, to solve this serious issue. In Brazil, and perhaps other countries as well, that is because there is a profound deficiency in medical training around pain management.

In order to be able to care for someone who is dying, the first thing you have to know is to what extent you can be there, how responsible you are for controlling your own reaction to their pain. That responsibility toward yourself is the measure of your ability to be responsible for caring for the life of any loved one. When you do not value life in this way, the person who is dying will be the first to see through you.

This is another revelation that comes with the dying process: you will be in a position to understand the truth contained in each past, present, and future choice in your own life. You will learn the true importance of each moment, and then strip away all of the masks, illusions, fears, fantasies, and things you've repressed. At the hour of your death, you become a veritable oracle, a seer of all truth.

This is another revelation that comes
with the dying process: you will be
in a position to understand the truth
contained in each past, present,
and future choice in your own life.

If you want some advice about your own life, ask someone who is dying. That wise breath of life, when it is near its end, surfaces into consciousness and illuminates their thoughts with a divine light, an outrageous lucidity; they manage to understand concepts and thought processes from before, during, and after life, all of those mysteries about which religious people say, "Only God knows."

When you face death, those truths are revealed in the eyes of whoever is there watching. If the person with you tells a lie, you will know. And if you are under the watchful eyes of someone who is dying, you can be sure they see all the truth in you. You may be an excellent doctor, nurse, journalist, lawyer, pharmacist, garbage collector, cook, and cleaner; you may be really good at a profession that does not require contact with other people's humanity, where it is enough to be highly proficient or have a set of professional skills. No one may notice that you are not a fully developed person, but in Palliative Care, that will enter the awareness of whoever you are caring for. It will be written in that person's eyes that you are wrong when you lie and tell them everything is okay.

If you feel incapable of being there for the patient, you can be certain that you are, in fact, incapable. If you feel unworthy, you need to figure out why. You will need to take charge of your own life in order to become worthy of being there for someone who is close to death.

To me, nothing is more sacred than being there for someone who is dying, because there will be no next time. Regardless of what faith tradition you profess, whether you embrace it or not, you die only once in this life. There is no rehearsal. You may have one, two, or three children, may have married five times, you may have done any number of things any number of times, but dying you will do only once. And only at that time. The degree of presence you have to develop in order to provide Palliative Care can only be achieved after committed, technical training, conscious physical activity in order to feel your own body, emotional therapy, and experiences that help you to find your own peace.

How can you help someone else find peace if you have no idea where to find your own? A diploma does not prove you've mastered the meaning of life, so do not be fooled by certificates. The importance you give to your own life cannot be measured in a job or college application. If you do not know where your own importance lies, then you are unlikely to be able to do anything for anyone else and, at the hour of their death, your presence might just be awkward.

The transformation starts when you realize you are capable of being present. Where the person who is dying is not made to feel they are a burden, a hindrance, a nuisance. They deserve the chance to discover that they are valuable to the person who is there for them, beside them. We all deserve that. To feel valuable, important, and loved, even when you are sick and dying.

The challenge for whoever wants to be there for a person who is dying is to know how to turn that person's feelings into something of value, to turn the sense of failing against the disease into a feeling of pride at having the courage to face the suffering of being finite. If the person who is dying feels valuable, in the sense of being important, of making a difference to their own life and to the life of whoever is looking after them, then they will honor that time.

Many people justify wanting to be there for people who are dying. They might say, "I want to be a volunteer in Hospice care, and help people as they die; I want to do Palliative Care to help people in their dying; I want to study thanatology to help people die." But what is true is just the opposite. Listen carefully: if you want to help people die, go look somewhere else. Go sell cigarettes, alcohol, drugs. Go spread violence and misery. That is what helps people to die.

To be there for someone who is dying,

you have to know how
to help them live

until the day of their death arrives.

Although many choose
to live as if dead,

all have the right to die alive.

When my turn comes, I want
my life to end in a good way:

on that day, I want to be alive.

THE LIVING DEAD

"An iron train is a mechanical thing,
but it runs through the night, the morning, the day, . . .
it ran through my life,
it became just feeling."

Adélia Prado

With terminally ill patients, it is common for everyone around the person who is dying to regard them as already dead—but there's a larger problem with the world around us that has little to do with physical disease.

Many people are not really fully alive, even though their bodies function properly. A devastating truth. Among those not fully alive are people who have buried the emotional, family, social, and spiritual dimensions of their lives. These are people who do not know how to relate—to others or to themselves—who have difficulty living well, without guilt or fear; people who would rather not believe, so as to avoid the risk of being disappointed, whether in others or in God; people who do not trust, do not give of themselves, who neither allow nor forgive, who do not give their blessing; living people who live as if they were dead. The dead are walking around freely in gyms, in bars, in television-ad family dinners, wasting their Sundays for months on end: people who complain about everything and everyone; people who perpetuate their own pain by numbing themselves with drugs, alcohol, or antidepressants, trying to protect themselves from the sadness of not being able to feel happy.

I see this in hospitals, especially in the doctors' room, the break rooms in the ward, and in the changing/scrub rooms. These are places populated by the dead walking around lost, finding no meaning in their work, day after day. In most hospitals and institutions that call themselves "health services," the strongest presence is the smell of the living dead. In large offices, I see people brimming with lifeless economic, political, and administrative rationality. They, too, have starved themselves of life and enriched themselves with death. The characteristic smell of death is prevalent wherever people have no chance to realize that they are alive, but wherever death really is, that is where life manifests itself.

The challenge to making someone feel alive is not to deny the process of death in them. Therefore, if you want to be there, working, experiencing the death of someone you love very much, these are the first challenges: to know who you are, what you are doing there, and how you are going to make that process as pain free as possible.

The next step is to know what ability you have to turn how that person sees themselves (a burden, a weight, a sea of fears and regrets) into something of value. If you feel lost in the midst of all this, then observe. In a wise line from the popular film *Pirates of the Caribbean*, a character throws some light on this tense moment: "You have to be lost to find a place that can't be found, otherwise everyone would know where it was." Take advantage of the time when you are lost. Being with someone who is dying will mean getting that lost feeling many times. It is not something to run from. It is in that space of time that you will discover uncharted paths within yourself to an incredible place—to life.

Being with someone who is dying
will mean getting that lost feeling
many times. It is not something
to run from. It is in that space
of time that you will discover
uncharted paths within yourself
to an incredible place—to life.

WE ALL COME TO THE END. WHAT IS
THE HARDEST PATH TO THAT DAY?

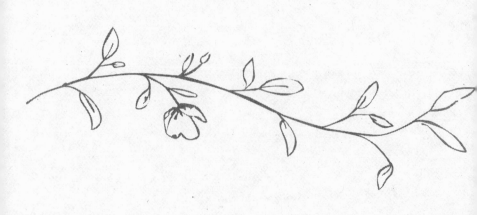

"The time has come—is and has already been here—when those who can, should save themselves."

Clarice Lispector

Time is a recurring theme when talking about death, about finiteness. When there is no more time, will there be time to be happy? When someone falls ill and needs to stop their time from passing so quickly, so that they can get treatment, time does not go by in seconds, minutes, hours; it passes in drips or pills. The intervals are marked between one medication and the next, between one doctor's visit and the next, between one test and the next. It is the time span of the saline dripping from the IV stand by the bed: every six hours, every eight hours. Time stretches on and does not pass.

As a doctor, I am privileged to work at society's two extremes: one, in an office at the Hospital Israelita Albert Einstein in São Paulo, where I meet patients who are socioeconomically well-off; and the other, at the Hospice connected to the Hospital das Clínicas, also in São Paulo, where I receive people who may arrive in a complexity of precarious medical and social support conditions—street people who come into my care. Two of the city's extremes joined by a single reality: they are sick and may be close to death.

It is clear to me that human suffering does not choose wealth or a certain number of diplomas, rubber stamps on a passport, whether plates are full or empty, or how many books are on the shelves. When you talk about expressions of suffering, the issues that motivate dying patients are exactly the same. The anger of a son fighting for his father's inheritance is the same as that of one fighting with his mother over a pension earned at half of a minimum wage. Despite the apparent social differences, people experience the same pain, the same loneliness, the same love of life, and also the same rage, the same guilt, the same fervent religious debates, the same behavior.

The difference between these two groups of patients, even when they receive all possible care within their respective worlds, is that the person with a lot of money may have a much more desolate experience in the process of dying. Having money leads people to believe that they can change anything, that they can restore their health by buying expensive medicines, expensive health professionals, expensive hospitals. But no amount of money in the world is going to protect you from dying when your time has come. Those who have enjoyed a wide range of opportunities in life enter the realm of regret much more readily when confronted by their own death. Those who have only ever had one choice in life—to survive—generally reach the end completely sure that they did the best they could with the opportunities they were offered.

At the Hospice at Hospital das Clínicas, there is no privacy, that chic name they invented for loneliness. There, our rooms are doubles. Death happens, and you are a witness to your roommate's death. Maybe to you that sounds morbid, but you become aware it will soon be your turn—and the lived experience of your neighbor's death can bring with it the realization that it might actually be a serene moment.

People who receive Palliative Care at the Hospice have the chance to pass in "first class." This metaphor of "passing" is often used to describe the process of dying. In his book *The Platform Ticket*, Derek Doyle, a Palliative Care specialist, tells the real stories of a doctor who works with people at the end of their lives. The expression "platform ticket" relates to the train station, where some board the train and others stay on the platform, helping others embark. We, the people who care for those who are dying, remain on the platform; we help them find their place and get comfortable, we load their luggage and we check that all those involved have said goodbye.

The expression "platform ticket" relates to the train station, where some board the train and others stay on the platform, helping others embark. We, the people who care for those who are dying, remain on the platform.

Everyone boards, but some board badly. As I mentioned earlier, unfortunately, people commonly associate Palliative Care with euthanasia. When I am called in to a assess a terminal patient, their relatives are afraid that I will do everything I can to put an end to the sufferer. To everyone involved—patient, family, and health team—I have to explain what caregiving means.

If the person really is at the end of their life and I write on the patient's chart, "Permission for natural death," the reaction is quite uncanny. The nurse will come to me and say "So, doctor, do we start sedation now?" And I have to start all over again, from the beginning, when all was darkness. How are babies born? Are they born having to be sedated? Okay, then! You don't need to be sedated to die either. Natural labor, natural delivery, natural life, natural death. Is that so hard to understand?

Yes, sometimes it is, and I have to draw a picture. It is much easier to get the family to understand than the nursing staff, nutritionists, speech therapists, physiotherapists and, worse still, the doctors. So you, dear reader, who are not from the health field, please forgive these poor creatures we call doctors, because we are given no training to talk about death at medical school. In fact, we do not even learn to talk about life! Our training is only in diseases. We are only good at talking about diseases, and then only in convoluted terms. Our vocabulary and lines of reasoning are extremely limited. Please show compassion and patience, because behind the gown and a few registration numbers, there beats a heart that suffers a lot too.

You start medical school with a sense of heroism and idealism ready to save lives, but experience teaches you that saving goes far beyond medication and surgery. What they try to teach us at medical school is that good doctors have to fend off death. Even though the doctor's work ought to be to promote health, we operate from a baseline of fear. Take tests! Walk five times a week, sleep, eat properly! Otherwise, you will die! Even though, of course, you are going to die whether you do all of those things or not. What we should be doing is warning people that, if you do those things, you will live better—and that should be a good enough reason.

It is a major challenge for doctors and healthcare workers to understand that when death ensues it is not a sign of failure. The doctor's true failure is when the patient they are treating does not live well. Many people are cured of cancer, but are completely unhappy to be alive. Why does that happen? What is the point of curing and controlling diseases if you cannot help patients understand that good health can be a bridge to enjoying meaningful experiences in their lives? The doctor's most important job in relation to their patients is not to neglect them while they are healthy—either when they are in good health or when death ensues.

THE SPIRITUAL DIMENSION
OF HUMAN SUFFERING

"When you touch someone, never touch just a body. I mean, do not forget that you are touching a person and that, in their body, is all the memory of their existence. And, more profoundly still, when you touch a body, remember that you are touching a Breath, that that Breath is the breath of someone with all their hang-ups and difficulties, and also that it is the great Breath of the Universe. So, when you touch a body, remember that you are touching a Temple."

Jean-Yves Leloup

In my day-to-day work with Palliative Care, the dying and their loved ones find themselves facing profound issues of human existence and spirituality. To talk about spirituality, you first have to first practice letting go; you have to give up everything you think you know in that regard. It is almost as if you were sitting in front of a sacred book, which is upside down, and trying to make the necessary mental adjustment so as to read it wrong-way-up, because the book cannot be moved and set right side up.

Over a decade ago, in the 2010 census, 92 percent of Brazilians claimed to follow a religion. And those who said they were not religious didn't necessarily not believe in God. Only 2 percent of the population declared no religion at all; among these, likely, are the true atheists. The majority believe in God and follow some form of religion; in fact, many hold to more than one. Because of that, Brazilians are often criticized for not being faithful to whatever the tradition sees as "God," be it God in Catholic, Protestant, Neo-Pentecostal, or other spiritual practices. The truth behind this "ecumenical" behavior, however, is that Brazilians—like so many the world over—are creatures in search of security and guarantees, a greater Someone or Something, a Being that will protect and support them and smooth out their path. Our culture, and many others from around the world, holds to a belief that everything can be made right by the advantages of certain religious behavior.

Most people come to realize the importance of their faith or religious tradition with their awareness that death is close, either because they are terminally ill or because a loved one is. It's then that they discover the possibility of entering into a relationship with God. Since I started working with Palliative Care, I have cared for hundreds of people, each one with a unique story, each one unvaryingly human. In all of those years, I have cared for people of all religions—Catholics, Neo-Pentecostals, Spiritists—and atheists.

Of all my patients—until I worked at the Hospice, where I cared for more than six hundred patients in less than four years—it was the atheists and humanists who were most serene in the process of dying. And to clarify, these were not people who converted to atheism, but those whose worldview was formed by a secular humanism that provides the foundation for secular humanist ethic.

And of those I've cared for facing death, it is the "converted atheists" who seem to experience the most spiritual suffering, the one who formerly believed in God, practiced a religion, then at some point God lost all credibility for them. They grew disappointed with their God, deciding they believed in no greater power, converting to atheism.

For those formed by or born into families who don't believe in a deity or higher power, I observed a heightened spirituality and a humanist ethic. They do good to themselves, to others, and to nature, and they practice that good with such respect that it is impossible not to be enchanted with the quality of their humanity. They do not believe in a deity that will save everything, but rather, do their part to save their own lives and the life of the planet they live on.

The atheists I worked with in the clinic fell ill, had cancer, did chemotherapy, radiotherapy, surgeries, came very close to dying or had relatives who were severely ill. Nonetheless, they displayed less spiritual suffering—something that may come from being at peace with the life they lived, and then they will be at peace with the end of life. It's a peace that those who come from some forms of religious fundamentalism cannot find, as they more often struggle with despair. Where they somehow believe their god is great enough to save them from hell and wrath, but cannot save them from death. Those who have trusted themselves to a religious belief system that tells them their god will spare them from death, or make the dying process easier, are bothered when they see their humanist atheist neighbors come through the entire process whole, even serene. No religion can prevent the presence of death. No god, no Catholic or Protestant, Jewish, Muslim, Buddhist, Hindu, or any other religion, can prevent the human body from coming to its end. Sometimes when I've talked about spirituality to hostile religious audiences, their indignation is clear: "How's that possible? How can people die well without believing in God?"

At the Hospice, I had the opportunity to witness the process of death in deeply religious people who also passed away very serenely. As a result, I came to understand a lot of things. Religion can either be a serious, even harmful, comorbidity or it can be a profound and effective instrument of healing.

Religion can either be a serious, even harmful, comorbidity or it can be a profound and effective instrument of healing.

A paper from the neuroscience community published in 2011 caught my attention as I thought about these different ways to live, to meet death. The paper described an area of the brain they called "God thought." Originally published under the title "The Price of Your Soul: How the Brain Decides Whether to 'Sell Out,'" the study evaluated the brain using functional magnetic resonance imaging (an imaging test that displays neurological activity in response to certain internal and external stimuli). The study evaluated brain activity of individuals responding to statements around what are usually considered sacred ideas or religious thoughts. The response was then recorded related to the area of the brain that responded to the stimulus of the phrase. In the second part of the study, the study subjects were offered money to change their opinion.

The first stage basically identified two important areas, one connected with cost-benefit assessment and the other, with moral values of right and wrong. When exposure to a "sacred" idea lit up the right-and-wrong area of the brain, the individual was less likely to accept a financial proposal to change their opinion than when the idea stimulated the cost-benefit area. That is, if the individual regarded what was sacred as a benefit, then it could be weighed against the corresponding costs and, depending on what was at stake (the life of a child, for instance), not even God was worth the cost.

The region of the brain associated with "God thoughts" is the part of the brain that becomes active when the person is encouraged to talk about God. If a person believes that God chastises those who disobey, the message to the brain relates not to "God," but to the person's idea that they would punish someone if they were God. The "words" of God recited by humans must be treated very carefully, because they say a great deal more about who quotes those words than about God. The true response to what is sacred is one that cannot be changed, despite a god who defies our expectations.

The paper also discussed how sacred values are changeable depending on what the holder believed others thought about them and their beliefs—that is to say, "doing good" because it impresses others is a common practice among people who call themselves devoutly religious. This might look like a person showing how charitable and generous they are, knowing they will receive "love" and praise for their "kindness." This behavior falls into the portion of the brain related to cost-benefit, where the benefit is related not to the sacred, but to the domain of social approval.

There are also those who do good for their own advantage. The benefits to be gained in another life, like "heaven," make people want to do good on Earth. Again, this attitude resides not in a sacred place in the brain, but is part of the weighing of advantages in the balance. This is not sacred; it relates to your brain as a business decision.

What is sacred in your brain, in your being, is what you do and what you believe in even when you receive no advantage by doing so, even at cost to yourself. Integrity is the measure of the things you believe in and give expression to. Those who think and feel differently from what they say and do are beings in disintegration.

Everyone's integrity hinges on what they think, and on its compatibility with what they say and do. When we are in the process of alignment, even when we have not yet accomplished this, it is a sign of wholeness.

I think of spirituality as an axis on which I move in relation to myself, to my life, to others, to society, to the Universe, to Nature, and to God. The drama of "religion" resides in the relationship with others and with God. The judgments and condemnations of religion, its dogmas, its social and institutional pressure, add toxic sentiments to this axis, hindering the natural flow of the Greater Good.

I think of spirituality as an axis on which I move in relation to myself, to my life, to others, to society, to the Universe, to Nature, and to God.

When people talk about religion, it is always related to a search for truth. Because of the nature of my work, I have studied many religions and have come to understand that some entail a belief in God while others do not. Buddhists and Jains do not believe in God; they believe in the divine, in the sacred, but not the existence of a creator, a higher mind who planned everything and put the design of the Universes into effect. In the search for truth, you find many people who experience religion in light of relationship with God, because, once you have established as true that God exists, the next step is to establish a relationship to God. Each religion has its own chemistry for this great endeavor most call their "relationship with God," a relationship that includes standards, rules of conduct, practices, texts, and scripts that will govern a group of faithful who are considered "special" and referred to as "chosen"—because they have chosen this religious path.

Humans have a strange habit of putting themselves into situations where they feel they are different and, when possible, superior to others—and religion fosters that perception of being chosen, of being favored, of being deserving, of being set apart approvingly from the rest of humankind—whom the given religious group disagrees with. In this favored position, people can develop a kind of obsession with knowledge brought by messengers. Compulsive reading, interminable courses, initiation processes, and torturous retreats lead, more and more, to a state of blindness to what is truly sacred.

Those most devoted to this acquisition of religious knowledge, to the "cognitive expansion" of religion, reach high-ranking positions in their religious organizations and come to regard themselves as messengers or priests. It is they, who, "spiritually" speaking, set themselves up as intermediaries in negotiation of others' conversations with God. These others, believing their own understanding to be limited, seek the version of truth and follow the intermediaries leading them whom they would most like to be true, saying, "Explain the truth to me."

The problem is that truth is not a concept; it is an experience. You can only enter into contact with spiritual truth when you transcend yourself, when you experience the truth. It makes no sense at all to declare, "I believe in God!" The individual who experiences the truth of the existence of God will say something different: "I know that God exists." Practical reason says I do not need to state that I believe that the sun rises every day; I know that the sun rises every day. I have no doubt at all in that regard.

People who know the truth about spirituality live that experience of transcendence; there is no need to prove anything, no need to convince anyone—and it is impossible to explain. Such people do not feel they are being attacked when someone doubts them. When you discuss religion in terms of conceptual truth, then it makes sense to argue, because you are then talking about rules, standards, policies, behavior, advantages and disadvantages, costs and benefits.

Another kind of relationship I observe people have with God is a power relationship, where people ask for something or tell God what to do. They want to persuade God to change his mind. They flatter, negotiate, make sacrifices, as if God were some kind of sadist, wanting people to travel miles on their knees, bleeding, in order to attain happiness or find peace. And when God does not behave as expected, a feeling of betrayal, of abandonment, of punishment wells up. The prayers of those who negotiate favors with God as we read between the lines sound like this: "I mean, look, I've got cancer, but it would be great if I was cured. I think you'll really be doing the right thing if you do what I ask. It'll go over really well with my family and my friends. I promise to print some flyers to hand out in the street and tell everyone what you did. So, I'm going to ask, you're going to grant my wish, and just wait and see how many people are going to believe in you if you play your part! Look, it's just a suggestion, because you know I do everything you say." This negotiation with God is nonsense.

Sometimes people think that God is deaf and demented. People will shout, desperately repeating the same prayer hundreds of times. But when you think like that, you are accessing that part of the brain labeled "God thought"—the deal-making mechanism in the brain that grows larger or smaller depending on the person's capacity to think critically. If you are not a critical thinker, negotiator, you end up getting into decision-making that is "way above your pay grade."

To questions of faith, different religions say very different things. Having faith is different from belief; I learned this from a very wise patient who, after a disastrous relationship with his family, went to live on the streets. Like many, his relationships with friends were better than those cultivated in the family. I asked him, "Francisco, do you believe in God?" His answer: "No, I don't believe in God. I have faith in God." My facial expression said, "Come again?" And he asked me, "Don't you understand?" I hadn't understood a thing, so he helped me. "You can believe in anything. I believe in demons, I believe in witches, but I only have faith in God."

That moment was an epiphany for me. You can believe in something, anything, but faith requires surrender. If you have faith in God, and faith that God will do the best for you no matter what happens, you will be certain that what happened was the best that could have happened. Whether it was disease, suffering and death, or healing, it was the best.

When you believe that God is going to cure you, then you are convinced that the best outcome in that process is for you to be cured. When you have faith, you put yourself in the position of being cared for, of being protected, you give yourself over to the good fortune of having a God, the right God for you, one who can guide you to your destiny, to what has to be lived through, wholeheartedly meaning it when you say to God, "Your will be done."

When you think about this process of faith as surrender, you see that there are few—very few—religious people. The spiritual experience is a lived truth, not a conceptual truth, and you can have an experience of transcendence regardless of whether or not you embrace a religion. To me, transcendence is an intense feeling of belonging, of becoming "one" with whatever awakes that feeling in you. That ocean, that sunset, that hug from someone you love, will only be complete because you are there and you belong to that moment, you are part of that ocean, that light, that sky, that breeze. There is no "past me" or "future me"—I am that moment, that present instant. When the moment and experience pass, we are different, transformed.

The ending of our life is an experience that has great power of transcendence. The experience of transcending is always sacred. It is like experiencing sea water: anywhere on the planet, it will always be salty. Whenever you experience transcendence, it will be sacred, always. If it were possible to enter a functional resonance imaging machine at a moment of transcendence, you can be sure that the area of your brain that would light up would correspond to what you hold sacred, valuable, good and true.

Maybe I shouldn't suggest that you question what you hold sacred, what you consider to be God. It's a dangerous venture to ask yourself about who and what God is, but it will happen when you face death—your own or the death of someone you love. So it is worth preparing yourself for that final assessment of faith: How does your faith stand when it is time to live your final hours and acknowledge that your mission is over? Be aware that suffering can trigger your transformation as a human being. It can be the moment when you come to understand a totally new version of God. If you think that each one of us, inside, has a kingdom of God, then each one of us has a completely unique, personal version of that divinity. And when you think you know everything about what is divine and sacred and you find yourself facing a person who is dying, then that God who lives within you will show you what truly is divine and sacred within you.

What is most dangerous, though, is when you think you know what is best as it relates to religion and, because of the certainty of your religious outlook, you interrupt the flow of relationship with the patient. That is a disaster. It would be a lot better if all palliative care personnel were simply lifelong humanist atheists, because pure atheists have at least an anthropological curiosity for other people's beliefs. True humanist atheists, often nonbelievers from the cradle, tend to be peace-loving souls who respect the beliefs and options of all others. Their MO: do not judge. They are curious. Not so with converted atheists; they are often fundamentalists, just like any religious person who ascribes to a narrow set of dogmas, and they wage wars to prove that God does not exist. Atheism by conversion is something I thus see as a religion, too, a religion that strives to prove that God does not exist.

Health personnel who want to convert patients to their own religion can be dangerous. When they are convinced that patients suffer for not choosing what they consider the right path, they are already declaring themselves incapable of understanding the nobility of that chosen path. There is always someone who thinks or says that a patient is dying because they have not accepted Jesus in their heart. When they think or say things like that, they are also declaring that Jesus has not entered their hearts, either, because if Jesus had, they would never act like that with someone suffering at their own imminent death. Jesus, Buddha, think of any guru or spiritual leader—they all died. Death is a sacred act.

A willingness to accept the patient's sacred beliefs and to try to enhance their understanding of them is the great challenge facing care for spirituality. That is why I say that, in order to care for someone who is dying, you have to shed your knowledge, your prejudices.

There is no one path that everyone must take, because each person you come across is a new prototype, a new universe. That universe is of such a magnitude, and at the same time is so unique and complex, that it lays bare your own pettiness. When you help the people who are close to patients, especially their loved ones, to see how grand the process of dying is, everything becomes clearer and flows better. It is possible to surrender calmly to this river flowing to the sea, without doubts, no hurry, no rush, no swimming against the current that is you, yourself. You accompany the pace of the person who is leaving. In that truly human interaction, religion is, in essence, a wonderful path that connects with something sacred within you. Perhaps God is not in the other person nor in you; maybe we are all "in" God.

Over time, caring for so many incredible people, I have come to realize that what makes this wheel of spirituality turn inside each of us is the Love and the Truth that we live with integrity: the Love that you feel, think, speak and live; the Truth you feel, think, speak and live. No matter what your religion, no matter whether you believe in God or not, if your spirituality is based on Love and Truth, lived and not just as concepts, no matter the path you choose, life will work out. Always.

REGRETS

"We suspend our disbelief.

And we are not alone."

Neil Peart

When confronting your own finiteness, what causes most anguish is the looking back. The awareness of imminent death makes you examine the life you have led and rethink your choices. There comes a time when you wonder: Did I take the right path? If I'd turned back, would I have been wealthier and would death have taken longer to arrive?

The first question you normally ask yourself when confronted with your own finiteness is, "Could there have been some way to avoid being here?" Ideas come to mind, like: If only I hadn't smoked, I wouldn't have lung cancer! If I hadn't driven drunk, I wouldn't be here now! If I had made more healthy choices, I wouldn't be here with blocked coronary arteries! If I hadn't been born into this family, I wouldn't have this disease!

While you still have time, you can make new choices, because regret comes when you don't have the opportunity to backtrack and choose the path you now recognize to be the right one. Once time has run out, the regret becomes almost a given: you have done something wrong and feel guilt. You may forget that, when you made that choice (which you now consider wrong), you didn't even realize you were going astray.

In her book *The Top Five Regrets of the Dying: A Life Transformed by the Dearly Departing*, Australian nurse Bronnie Ware tells of her experience with those the medical community calls "terminal patients," people at the end stage of life. In her home visits and conversations with people at death's door, she began to see that regret was a recurrent theme. Bronnie describes five of the greatest regrets expressed by people who are dying. These are the regrets I also see, day after day, in my patients, and her description is exactly right.

The first of these regrets is, "I wish I'd had the courage to live a life true to myself, not the life others expected of me." As death approaches and people reflect on the time they wasted, many say they would like to take back the time they devoted to others, when they did things they believed were for the good of others. Except no one asked them to do any of that; people devote themselves to others because they want to, for the noblest—or the most selfish—reasons imaginable.

Nearly always, when you do something to please someone else, you do it in the belief that you are contributing to their happiness. Between the lines, however, these choices you make validate your own importance in that someone's life. Just think about it: using your time to make yourself important in another person's life is a tormenting way to live. If you can be yourself and if that makes you loved for what you are, then that is happiness, that is plenitude. Conversely, if you have to turn yourself into someone else in order to be loved, something is wrong. You will almost certainly regret it. It's a dangerous path when you cannot be what you pretend to be for others.

When you are accompanying someone as they are dying, it is fundamental to understand that the person is not dying so that you can feel useful. That is not the purpose. They are not there to convince you that you are good for something. Being there for someone who is dying is a much greater act than your whole existence. Your existence exists so that you exist; it is as simple as breathing.

Over the course of your life, however, you choose "third party" beneficiaries of your decisions, offering them to people who never asked to be chosen. If you decide, for example, I'm going to work hard, because I want to give my children the best, I'm not going to eat or sleep; I'm going to work from sun up to sundown to pay for a really expensive school, so that they can be doctors, engineers, lawyers. And then, when your child wants to be an artist, or to travel and see the world, you fail to honor your children's decisions or don't even believe they are discerning enough to make them. You do not discuss it with them, nor do you look for ways that everyone can work together toward doing what they really want. When they decide on a different path from what you imagined for them, your frustration comes out in an indignant "What do you mean? And I sacrificed so much for you! You're so ungrateful!"

I once cared for a woman with advanced dementia who had spent more than twenty years bedridden, dependent on her daughter's care. The daughter screamed that her mother could not die. "I gave my life for her! When I was twenty, all set to get married, the invitations had been sent out, the church was ready, everything paid for, she said to me, 'You're not going to abandon me, are you? Now, when I'm old and sick?'" So the daughter gave it all up: canceled the wedding, stopped studying, all to care for her mother. Thirty-five years went by. The woman asked herself how dare her mother die, after she had given up the best part of her life for her. What right did she have to die? To her, of course, her mother could not die. In despair, she begged me, "Treat her, give her morphine, she can't die! Intubate her, do everything, because she has to live. My life depends on it."

That is a dramatic story, one of extreme suffering. When the mother demanded that her daughter give up her own life, the daughter did not know how to tell her she could care for her in other ways. She accepted the blackmail and regretted it, but the regret came too late and became a lament—but by then, there was no going back.

Don't we all "interpret" similar requests (even if not quite as dramatic as this one) and fail to live our own lives so as to meet someone else's expectations of us? The truth is that you lose count of the times when you have made decisions to please others—and, in the end, will have to weigh those choices in the balance.

> The truth is that you lose count of the times when you have made decisions to please others—and, in the end, will have to weigh those choices in the balance.

One frequently hears harsh criticism of hospitals and clinics "abandoning" the elderly on their death beds. Nonetheless, it is important not to jump to conclusions about patients' loneliness in hospitals. Many people think that, because a person has cancer or is more than sixty years old, they are suddenly saints deserving worship and love from the whole family. That is not how life works, though. The quality of your relationships is something you yourself cultivate, and how you cultivate it will determine whether or not you will enjoy good company—or be alone—at the end of your life. What is the real story behind each abandonment? Who is that person in the hospital? Who will each of us be in the hospital? Will you be a bottomless well that just gave and gave and never received anything back in return? If you were an empty well in life, you will continue to be so at death's door. It will be very hard to reconstruct relationships and live meaningful memories after such a long, difficult journey, traveled in what was actually a harmful manner.

In the end, you may be able to build a relationship with healthcare personnel. Many people die receiving love from their caregivers. It is quite common for people on their hospital bed, people who were considered difficult their whole lives, to end up forging very beautiful bonds with us, their palliative care professionals and caregivers.

All the same, the moment someone on their deathbed understands that they have made decisions to make other people happy—people who never asked for anything of the sort or, worse still, were dissatisfied with those decisions—then regret sets in and is too painful for words, and that is a pain no amount of morphine can dull.

FORTHRIGHT FEELINGS

> "Where love hurts me is under my arm, in a hollow between
>   my ribs.
>
> How it reaches my heart is down that sloping path.
>
> I put love in the grinder with ashes and red nuts and
>
> I pound it. I steep it,
>
> I shape it into a poultice
>
> And put it on the wound."

Adélia Prado

Another regret nurse Bronnie Ware talks about in her book and which I see in my day-to-day practice has to do with hiding or holding back feelings. Bronnie mentions "love" as the specific feeling, but I extend the definition to feelings in the general sense, even "bad" feelings.

We are brought up and taught to control how we express our feelings. For that purpose, we use masks and disguises. In order to be accepted, heard, and understood, we learn how to hide much of what we feel. We come to believe that hiding our feelings can protect us. Over the course of life, living with others, you feel a lot of pain, which is why you develop strategies to defend yourself from the next hurt. "I did that and got hurt" and "I don't want it to happen again" are recurrent thoughts we have all had.

Ridiculously, we act as if everyone we meet is a clone of that first person who hurt us. There is a tendency to believe that people are all the same. Some people think the whole world is out to get them. That's not so. Not even our enemies would waste their energy on such a mission. We all want to be happy. Even those who do us wrong want the same thing we do—a happy life, full of accomplishments. That may be the most liberating thing that Buddhist philosophy has taught me: everyone just wants to be happy. The worst and the best human beings have that desire in common with me. I have learned that no one in the world was born just to make me unhappy.

When you are afraid to expose yourself, you do not say what you feel; you wear a mask. Over the course of a lifetime, you collect masks; you use those best suited to your style. If you want to be accepted, you use the attentive, good guy mask; you are always ready to help, everyone can rely on you. You are loved.

Then the time comes when you take off the mask and everyone sees you. You are naked, body and soul. If you were good just to please others, then the time will come to understand that you have to be good for real, for you, if you are to face the loneliness of life's ending. In one way or another, the truth always comes out in your relationships: even when you do not realize you are pretending, the other person ultimately perceives it—and when that happens, you are alone. There are many stories like that in a hospital, stories of people who helped others and who now find themselves there, alone. But they helped others with one single motive: to feel secure, not to build relationships.

The need for emotional security is a black hole. You can find everything in that black hole except true affection. You put on the friendly mask and, ultimately, the result is the reverse of your chosen style, you're closed off. Being emotionally undemonstrative as a defense strategy leads to regret, because you live with intense inner experiences and feelings—and you keep them imprisoned inside yourself. By depriving others of the chance to share in your emotional ups and downs, you ignore the fact that it is those encounters that change you: navigating your own expectations, your own thoughts, the insight gained from self-help books or revelations that dawn on you during a lecture—none of that helps if they are not shared with others.

The inner world does not offer much potential for change. What does have that potential for change are true encounters with others, because other people may offer the keys to some of the closed doors within you, doors that guard major revelations and secrets about yourself. Maybe I hold the key to open your heart in some way. Or maybe I hold the key to open your anger compartment: when you see me, all you can think about is how unbearable I am. And maybe it's not so enjoyable to be around me, because I opened the secret door to your anger.

Yet, in the same way, there are people who open up places within you to reveal love, peace, and joy. All of those emotions already inhabit your heart; I cannot bring you anything you do not already possess. Many authors, writers, thinkers have said that, but even more incredible is when it happens right in front of your eyes, right in your own heart. I can bring out something you may not yet know you have, because I have the key—I or someone else—but it comes from engaging someone outside you, outside ourselves.

All of those emotions already inhabit
your heart; I cannot bring you
anything you do not already possess.

This is made clear to me when my patients approach their encounter with the dying process. All of us have within us a heightened awareness of our various feelings through death. If I manage to open the right door, everyone will find the same things I do. What is different for each of us, and where we can affect change, is in the degree to which we express emotion and, if you are the instrument of that change, your life feels full—whether these emotions are good or not.

Making value judgments about what you feel—trying to convince yourself that a feeling is good or not good—can be very dangerous in the final moments. "Should I wish my mother would die?," "Am I allowed to feel hatred for my father?," "I want this person, who I should love so much, to die!" These kinds of emotions well up spontaneously, uncontrollably, and you try, by your own willpower, to make a conscious decision about whether they are good or bad, whether you can allow yourself to feel them or not. We usually decide it is normal, kind, and pleasant to demonstrate good emotion, and that showing bad emotion is none of those things. Often though, it is through bad emotion that change really happens. We do not always reach people, nor are we reached, by the gentle path of joy. I am not saying that suffering is the only possible way, but its ability to bring change may quite possibly be indisputable.

The great human dramas are all very similar. "I'm upset at most of the people here, but nobody knows it" is one of them. "I'm really angry with you, but I'm not going to tell you" is another. "I don't want to talk about it, because I can't. I'm no good with conflict" is just as common. When you show no emotion, it gets bottled up inside you. Emotional energy does not simply evaporate, especially when the feelings arise in the context of close relationships. The process of trying to cure bad feelings, of doing a kind of inner recycling, produces toxic waste even as we often fail to realize it. The most healing thing you can do is give honest expression to what you feel.

It should also be understood that having enemies is not all bad. Sometimes it is through them that you find the strength and courage to overcome obstacles. Your friends love you as you are. You think you're giving your best to your friends, but often it is enemies who demand the best of us. Everyone wants to be happier, more successful, stronger, more everything. With your enemies, you have to show unbelievable strength. Conflict confronts you with difficult feelings and people who may truly cause you harm. These confrontations can be a great catalyst for change, they push you to discover the power that lies within you. I am not talking about revenge, but rather the ability to take control of your inner strength.

Even when you show emotions that are hard to deal with, you offer the person on the other side of the ring the opportunity to change too. What is beautiful is that, by revealing more of yourself, you also open yourself up to change. When you acknowledge and feel your pain, then you can heal the wounded soul trapped inside the hurt. Those who survive this kind of open heartedness just carry scars; those who ignore their open wounds die badly.

When you acknowledge and feel your pain, then you can heal the wounded soul trapped inside the hurt.

You will come to the end of the road, facing that final wall, regretting not having shown affection for people who may have departed earlier—a mother, a son, a wife. Regret over missed opportunities to show what you really feel will make itself felt in full force at the end of life. If there is still time to demonstrate that affection, however, and if you do so—ah, that is an amazingly beautiful experience!

WORKING TO LIVE, LIVING TO WORK

*"And if you cannot work with love,
but only with distaste,
it is better that you leave your work
and sit at the gate of the temple
and take alms from those who work with joy."*

Gibran Khalil Gibran

Another regret dying patients express is having worked too much. If your work enables you to make the world better, even if only a little and for only a few people, if you throw yourself into that work with real change-making energy and you find fulfillment, then the course you have chosen will make sense, even though it takes a lot of effort.

Everyone thinks of a lifetime as a list of achievements. There are people for whom living means owning things; they work like crazy to have, to accumulate, and they accumulate not just material things, but also resentment and trauma. They end up with a lot of stuff at the end, including problems. Real regret, however, comes from needing to wear masks in order to survive at work. When who you are at work is not who you are in your personal life, then you are in trouble. You picture yourself at work, and you do not recognize that person, but you justify it: "That person working there is another being, there to perform that function; I am someone else." You are far away, not there inside that jacket, that suit, that tie, those shoes.

If you could learn how to be yourself wearing those shoes, then you could get your feet on the ground before it is too late, and you could no longer tell the sole of your foot from the sole of your shoe.

It isn't just those who wear the suit and tie or an elegant dress, the ones who don a company uniform or a doctor's gown at work are unhappy too. A lot of artists, even in a creative environment, are still terribly unhappy. We judge other people's jobs, but the truth is that each us knows best the weight of our own burden. Some people think others' lives are better than theirs, but that is not always true. When you accept a job that cuts you off from your true self, you will feel you are wasting time, particularly if you prefer your true self to your work self.

It is also risky to want to be job-defined, especially if you can only see yourself as somebody associated with your work. Such people may have incredible careers, but disastrous personal lives. Retirement for them is tantamount to dying. They play their role much more fluidly in the work environment than in their "real" lives.

This often happens among health professionals—many are thoroughly unhappy in their personal lives because they work in the health field. Although they follow, to the letter, the universal code that you should do unto others what you would have them do unto you, there is often something sick about the act of caring, of giving and being useful. They do unto others what they are incapable of doing unto themselves— and that is a very poor rule.

In those circles, you are forever hearing remarks like, "Where I work, there's a mother who's losing her child. How can I complain about my life? Hers is a lot worse than mine." Health professionals who set themselves up as saviors, caregivers, even if as volunteers, only transfer something external to others. They do not connect with others. There is a barrier to any genuine relationship. They are present in the patient's life, but wear a fairy godmother mask: they only give and will not allow themselves to receive. As a result, they lose the chance for any real encounter with the person they are caring for and, at the end of the day, they are exhausted.

When health professionals are truly present in their work and open themselves up to the possibility of shared learning and change, they feel renewed at the end of the day.

Sometimes I get to the end of my day tired out: I leave home at six in the morning and usually get home after eleven at night, but my energy level tends to stay high—and I am always fulfilled, not fragmented. Of course, I get physically tired, just like anyone else who has to cross São Paulo city (hours in traffic, on double alert for fear of violence), but I never tire of caring, working, doing something for others and staying open and willing to be changed.

Certainly there are days when I do not feel like opening up. On those days, when some personal matter takes precedence, I am the first to recognize the signs and alter my agenda accordingly. If I cannot be there for others, if I need time to connect with myself, then I am at peace with that decision. I do therapy, meditation, art, poetry. Any activity that can connect me with the essence of who I am teaches me and assures me the world will go on turning even if I am not pushing. That is a challenge for caregivers who think things will only work out if they are controlling them. Those people, when death approaches, feel as though life owes them something.

Work issues are a common thread running through this whole crisis of dying, but why? How much of your lifetime do you spend at work? Most of us spend at least eight hours a day working, about a third of our time, not to mention extra activities we partake in, trying to improve our work performance. You meditate to improve attention, do physical exercise to feel better, and all in order to work more. Although that may be the right road, it can be traveled for the wrong reasons.

Doing good things in order to be happy in life is different from doing good things to score points at work. If you choose self-care not for the pleasure of having a massage, but in order to ease back pain and thus be able to work the next day, then perhaps there is something wrong with your logic. People who live for the sake of work generally regret it, particularly if the driving force is fear—the cancer in humankind—fear of not having money, fear of your children not going to a good school, fear of having nowhere to live. Such people hide behind the age-old justification: "I have to work." Then they plow ahead, believing they are helping someone who never asked for that help. What are they going to do when the wall rears up in front of them?

Sometimes I imagine a mirror on my wall, where I will have to look into my own eyes and ask myself, "What now? How did you get here?" I will have to explain to myself the path I took.

Sometimes I imagine a mirror on my wall, where I will have to look into my own eyes and ask myself, "What now? How did you get here?" I will have to explain to myself the path I took. I will not have to explain it to my son, to my parents, or to my friends. I will not have to explain it to my boss or my colleagues who wanted to pull the rug out from under me. In the end, I will be alone with myself, no intermediaries. I have to understand my death because it is mine. The wall that is my death is not my son's, nor my husband's, nor my father's, my mother's, my boss's. The path is mine.

The same mirror reasoning relates to work. This line of questioning can change your life before you fall ill, before you actually run into death. It does not take long to change your life. The issue of work also relates to money, of course: everything you get out of your work has the same energy you put into it.

Some years ago, a nurse friend was promoted to a leadership position at a large hospital. The only thing I could think of to say to her was, "Careful what you do with the life ahead of you." Knowing she was good and purehearted, I felt for her—after all, I knew that, although her bank account would grow, the life in store for her would bring more sadness and problems. She might have to spend her new salary on therapy or medication or, even more seriously, on the chemotherapy she may have to undergo two years later.

The energy generated from a job that makes no sense to your life is bad energy too. With the extra money, you will buy food that will go bad quicker, a car that will break down all the time; you will join a gym that you have no time to go to, buy clothes you will not use, take courses you will forget. When you look at your life and realize you have spent it buying things that do not help you live a better life, maybe there is something wrong with where that money came from. If you earn a fortune and buy a car only to arrive home looking like a zombie, something is wrong.

ELECTIVE AFFINITIES

"Who is a friend? Another self."

Zeno of Elea

The fourth regret Bronnie Ware talked about in her book has to do with spending more time with friends.

When Facebook was invented, with it came a sense of community. I am someone who, when I see someone's Facebook page, feel close to that friend. I make good use of it as a tool and take full advantage of any time I can share with people who are dear to me, but geographically distant. There are people that I love an awful lot, but my life does not allow me to be physically close to them at the moment. I cherish the photos of their children growing, the important events, our shared taste in music and poetry and, one way or another, I feel part of that parallel universe. At some level within me, I really do connect with those people.

However, I think it is also vital to spend time with friends. With them, you can build more honest, transparent relationships—something that is not always possible with family. With friends, you can say, "I didn't like what you did"—and that is all right, because they can handle the criticism. When you are with friends, you want your choices and feelings to be respected, and they are. Your family are not always the most pleasant people in the world, or necessarily the people you want to live with. You can count those who like to spend Christmas with relatives on one hand—many people do it as an obligation, but not much enjoyment.

Unfortunately, you have more time on your hands when you are ill. You want friends to keep you company, those who see you despite the disease, despite the suffering. You want to see yourself in their eyes, because in their gaze you reencounter your own story, your importance in the world. Being with friends, you often experience a state of pleasant, lighthearted presence. Close to death, regret for not having devoted more time to them hits hard. Regretfully, you think you had free time your whole life, but in fact you did not.

At life's end, there are also some regrets that are a pure waste of time; it makes no sense for them to be cause for suffering. Often, you chose a path that you did not know would be bad; you do now and you regret it. It is like playing the lottery and saying, "I chose forty-four, but it came up forty-five. What was I thinking not to have chosen forty-five!" The simple truth is that you did not choose forty-five because you thought forty-four was going to win! It is not fair to blame yourself for past actions in light of what you know now. When you start with that "I should have" or "I could have" drama, it is time to look in the mirror and say, "Don't beat yourself up like that. You made a sound decision based on what you knew at the time." You could perhaps say, "If I had known it was going to go wrong, I would have done differently," but you did not know, you could not have known.

Being present in every decision in your life, in your thoughts, feelings, voice, and attitude can prevent some of these regrets, but the decision you made on any given occasion was the one you thought best at the time.

MAKING YOURSELF HAPPY

"No one can make us unhappy, only ourselves."

St. John Chrysostom

The last regret, which to me summarizes all the others, is this: I should have made myself a happier person. Many people think a state of happiness is simple joy and pleasure, but a state of complete happiness is often attained after overcoming particularly difficult times in life—heavy, anxious times we go through with blood, sweat, and tears, but that we come out of whole, intact, covered in scars, but survivors, better and stronger than before. That kind of overcoming brings with it a state of complete happiness.

There is a connection between helping someone who is dying and making yourself a happier person. It entails seeing that person as complete and yourself as their equal—because we are dying too. When you help someone, when you are there for them, you are beside them, not inside them. When you are only inside your own suffering, then you use that person to fulfill your own needs. What I am saying sounds cruel, but it is very true. Beware—whether you are a social worker, nurse, doctor, son, or spouse—that you are not caring for someone in order to become them, and thus use that person to give meaning to your choices.

You need to have compassion in order to be present in the sacred space of relationship, of encounter.

So what can you do in order not to regret it all later? Everyone knows the road to regret, but how do you go about not having regrets to begin with? I do not think there is a formula or step-by-step manual, but one book that did change me in this regard was *The Four Agreements* by the Mexican author Don Miguel Ruiz.

The first agreement he suggests is to be impeccable with your use of words. Words have much greater power to change and to destroy than any medical treatment, far greater than any surgery or medicine, and they have even more power when they find a voice. When you give voice to something you believe in, the words take on something of yourself. I do not mean just the good words. Sometimes it is necessary to say, "What you did was not good!" Depending on how you say it, though, the person receiving the criticism may agree with you or be profoundly offended.

If you are unable to find the right words, keep quiet. Silence has just as much power as words. When I am irritated, I prefer to be quiet, and if anyone asks, "Aren't you going to say anything?," I answer carefully, "I don't have anything good to say at the moment." I assure you, there is no beating a silence of that magnitude. It is a silence full of words that must not be said, that no one wants to say. It is the most appropriate fire extinguisher for that kind of fire. To put out a forest fire, you need water, an electrical fire takes foam, and a fire of words calls for silence.

The second agreement is not to jump to conclusions. If I pass you on the street and don't say hello, you may think, Did I say something I shouldn't have said the last time we met? The worst arguments start with the words: "I assumed that you, I thought that you. . . ." That web of conclusions envelops and suffocates you even as it excludes the other person from the story. The people around you become merely characters in crazy tales you tell, often perversely, in your own mind. The simplest way to handle it would be to say, "Ana, why didn't you say hello to me yesterday?" My answer might be totally unthinkable to a mind bent on twisting reality: "Look, I'm sorry, I was so late, so distracted, I didn't see you!" Everything might be so much simpler than you imagine.

The third agreement Ruiz discusses is not to take anything personally. This is really difficult. People with poor self-esteem believe that everyone else thinks terrible things about them. Everyone else, meanwhile, is simply living their own lives, but some people imagine others spend their time thinking about how unimportant they are. Low self-esteem can be just a twisted way of being self-centered. You are not special enough for everyone to be thinking about you—one way or another. The world does not turn on your navel, or in spite of it. The opposite is also true: praise should not be taken personally. If someone thinks you are important and interesting, that does not necessarily have anything to do with you. It has to do with a key you hold that opens the door to well-being in the person giving the praise. Simple as that, once again. Jumping to conclusions and taking things, good or bad, personally means you often make wrong decisions, which will lead you to regret.

"Always do your best" is the fourth agreement. Sometimes your best is to be grumpy or not to leave the house or to be annoyed. If I have a bad day, when I get home, I warn my children, my friends, my love: I am having a bad day. Mysteriously, the dishes get washed, my coffee or tea is ready, someone puts my favorite music on. I get smiles and kindness. Be aware of how you feel and let others know; it works like a charm.

Some years ago, I coordinated a home care team. I proposed a new routine: when people got to work, they were to choose a badge that would indicate how they felt that day. That badge was placed on their ID tag or the internal notice board that listed all the staff's names. The badges were color coded: green for "okay," yellow for "so-so," red for "not now!"

I am unbearably good-humored, but I have my off days too. When I chose red, I knew that simple gesture could make my whole day go differently. Someone passing my desk might smile timidly and say, "I wanted to talk to you about something today, but maybe tomorrow would be better." Friendly notes would appear, a coffee, a tea, half-smiles, waves from a distance. It was magic. And you could change your badge throughout the day. A day that started out badly was not fated to end badly—and it was very rare for someone to spend the whole day with a red badge.

When I chose a badge, I accepted that it was for my reasons. Doing your best means paying attention to what state you are in, so that you can do your best. When you are in a bad state, it is best not to do anything, to shut up or put out a warning that you are not all right. It improves your life—and its ending—to understand that, in everything you did, right or wrong, you were trying to get things right. You were giving your best. Today you may think you could have done it all differently, taken another path, but at the time, you gave your best.

It improves your life—and its ending—to understand that, in everything you did, right or wrong, you were trying to get things right. You were giving your best.

Perhaps the easiest way to live well would be to incorporate the following five small things into your daily life: show emotion, allow yourself to be with friends, make yourself happy, make your own choices, and work at something that makes sense in your life time and not just during work time. No regrets.

"I have got my leave! Bid me farewell, my brothers! I bow to you all and take my departure. Here I give back the key to my door—and I give up all claims to my house. I only ask for last kind words from you. We were neighbors for a long time, but I received more than I could give. Now the day has dawned and the lamp that lit my dark corner has gone out. A summons has come and I am ready for my journey."

Rabindranath Tagore

OUR EVERYDAY DEATHS

"Everything must be being what it is."

Clarice Lispector

You spend your life trying to learn how to win. You look for countless courses, books, techniques for how to win people over and obtain material things, benefits, and advantages. There are any number of lessons on the art of winning, but what about the art of losing?

No one wants to talk about that, but the truth is that you spend a lot of your life suffering badly when you lose things, people, situations, dreams. You have thousands of reasons to dream, but when you lose your dreams, you should not lose your head. You spend your life looking for advice about how to win the love of your life, the job of a lifetime. I don't think anyone would sign up for a course called "How to Lose Well" or "How to Lose Better in Life."

However, knowing how to lose is the art of those who have managed to enjoy to the fullest everything they have gained in life.

Every existential loss, every symbolic death, whether of a relationship, a job, or a certainty, needs to be made sense of in at least three ways. The first has to do with forgiving, yourself and others. The second is knowing that whatever happened that was good in that situation will not be forgotten. The third is the certainty that you made a difference in the time you had, you left a legacy, made a mark that changed that person or situation that will now be gone from your life.

Acceptance of loss has a vital function in your ongoing life.

Unless it is certain that something has ended, it is difficult to embark on another project, another relationship, another job. You are trapped in a "should have, could have" limbo, stuck in the "What if . . . ?" It is as though you press pause on your life between breathing out and breathing in: the air has gone out of your lungs, but you have not let the new air in because you are still holding your breath.

That "interval" is what we should fear the most and avoid the most. When you end a relationship, but cannot accept that it is over, you are stuck in an interval. You become an emotional zombie. Relationships die, but you try to keep them alive. And those relationships decay inside you, contaminating all the others. You believe it would be harder to endure the loss than to turn up at the wake, but actually it is much easier to get over loss than to breathe the putrid air of emotional decay.

These symbolic losses are deaths that can be harder to deal with than actually dying. There is no arguing with real death, but a symbolic death—of a relationship, a job, a career—sometimes gives the impression of not really being a death. Something lives on and we trick ourselves into believing it will somehow be possible to resuscitate that relationship, that career, that certainty. The moment you understand death is happening, that is also a wall, the wall of that relationship, that job, that time, that phase of your life. You come to the wall and you cannot jump over it or go around it; you have to look at it and acknowledge that this death, this ending exists.

You will only manage to move on to the next stage once you have confirmed one of these three conditions: that you have forgiven, that you have left your mark, or that you carry the experience with you and can draw possible lessons from it. I see this in how mourning processes play out when they are not associated with an actual death.

The first condition involves asking if there is anything to regret, anything that contributed to that death: something you said that you should not have, or something you should have said that you failed to. If the answer is yes, then you feel responsible in making that death happen and there is regret.

The second thing to ask when moving on from a loss is whether you will be forgotten. This happens especially with ex-wives and ex-husbands. Some do everything possible to make themselves eternally present; they do not want to be forgotten, ever, but all they leave to be remembered by are deep traces of hatred and revenge. It would be freeing for them if they made themselves memorable not for the harm they caused, but the good.

Meeting the third condition can afford an experience of immortality. You move on, but you leave something of your essence, your story, in the time and space you shared with that person who has gone out of your life.

Let's take the end of a work relationship. This kind of death can be good, depending on who decides its end. When you resign, the end is easier. You face the wall, you understand that a stage has come to an end, and right away you scan new horizons—a sabbatical, a new field of work, a new position with higher earnings or more power. That job will die according to plan; everything is under control. It hurts more to be dismissed, and poses the question of how to live with something that was terminated against your wishes.

The greatest suffering happens when you gaze at your own navel and realize that it is not the center of the world. The best way to stay alive, despite these deaths that occur in the course of your life, is to be present in them. If you live and love to the fullest, then you can let things and people go on their way. If you have experienced all that the relationship has to give, then you are free. There is nothing holding you, no unfinished business. Giving yourself completely to the experience makes it possible to let go. When you entered the relationship, the job, the situation, you brought the best of yourself; you changed, you immersed yourself in that encounter, and then the time came for it to end. So you go on your way, taking what you have learned with you, and that will enable you to enter into another relationship, another job, another career, another dream of a lifetime.

If you live and love to the fullest, then you can let things and people go on their way. If you have experienced all that the relationship has to give, then you are free. There is nothing holding you, no unfinished business.

Trying to control the situation only prevents you from experiencing that full engagement. When this is lacking, you are unable to evolve or grow, and instead get tied up in that knot of expectation, in that bind of believing the encounter was supposed to be forever when, in fact, the "forever" encounter never actually happened. The job that was supposed to last forever never made anyone happy forever. The career that was to be forever never had the potential for you to leave a legacy. Whenever you wish something would last forever, you run the risk of it not making you happy today simply because you believe it will make you happy in the future. You are always building, always renovating, thinking about the future: when the company will be yours, everything will be different. You make love to someone who is not good for you at the moment, but after the wedding, you think all that will change. When you have children, it will be different. You are forever thinking that it will be different one day, but not now—and then death intervenes, putting an end to both present and future.

The past dies from regret over time for living a life wasted on poor choices. You can deal well with everyday deaths if you stop trying to obsessively plan only for a happy future.

Today, if you were fired from your job, would the life you lived at work have been worth it? Or would you look back and say, "Good grief, what a mess! I really suffered! Marriage, job—I gave years of my life to all of that and I wasn't even appreciated! Look what it did to me! I shouldn't have done it, I shouldn't, I shouldn't!" Then you'd be left with the thought that you wasted your life, trashed years of living. It is the last impression that stays with you, not the first. You might meet the most incredible person you have ever met and marry them, only to discover they really disappoint you. Eventually, that person becomes unrecognizable to you, a monster. The impression you are left with is the lasting one.

So what happened in the interval between that person being incredible and morphing into a monster? Or could it all have been just a mistake caused by you jumping to conclusions and taking things personally? Did you choose your words with impeccable care or did you use words that would bring out the devil in any angel? Did you really give your best and find a way to accept the best from the other person, even though they failed to live up to your expectations? How did that encounter transform you? Who are you after that experience? That is the legacy I am talking about. If you end a relationship by erasing all the time you spent with that person, then you are choosing to destroy part of your own life. That is the real dilemma we all face when experiencing symbolic losses.

The experience of loss or the expectation of loss, even when that loss never actually happens, will only become less painful if, as it is happening, you engage fully, change in the process, and, if possible, manage to change the other person. That is why it is so important to think very carefully before getting—and settling—into a relationship, mainly because nothing is final except past experience; no relationship, no job, no choice. Nothing is final, everything ends; whether well or badly will depend on how you guide your life through each of these processes. If they end badly, it takes even more work to start over again.

The first step in learning to lose is accepting that you have lost. What is over, is over; there are no eternal do-overs. Facing the end honestly is something you develop over the course of your life; you prepare to learn to see the truth. I do not mean learning to see a new beginning, but seeing the truth lovingly, without resentment. To be loving with someone who has betrayed you, a boss who humiliated you, a job that makes people's lives worse, you must first be compassionate with yourself. You must understand that you took that attitude, made that choice, decided to be with that toxic person because, at that time, that was as far as you could see.

So rather than hating the person who harmed you, you should be compassionate with yourself for having gone through that experience. In one way or another, it may turn you into someone better, happier, less bitter, more capable of other relationships or another job. No one wants to end up with someone who stays perpetually emotionally immature.

When the reality of death is not accepted, mourning gets complicated; but when lesser deaths are not accepted, that produces emotional immaturity: you are incapable of new relationships, new jobs, new projects, because you have erased yourself with the outcome of the previous experience. You choose to be a victim. And you should never do that.

When you make yourself the victim in an ending, when you continue to make choices for the wrong reasons, the ending will almost certainly be painful. If you choose a path to please others, if you do something just to feel loved and accepted, then when the end approaches, you will be at war with yourself. The war will be for power, and hinges on being acknowledged for your "sacrifice." Often, you get yourself into an emotional bind or a dead-end job because you believed it when they said, "This project cannot be done without you," or "I cannot live without you," or "You are of the utmost importance." Your ego soars as you likely embark on a journey of epic failure which, just around the corner, will push you into the abyss.

You know you are at the abyss and yet you still decide to take a step deeper in. You do that all too often in life. You can see that the ship is going down, you want to get off, but then you make that false effort. "No, this time I'm in charge," you tell yourself. "This time it's going to be all right, because I am in command; this relationship depends on me to work; this family depends on me and I'm going to make it work." Except you are reducing other people to mere characters in your story, characters that you put there hoping they would behave as you planned. "You're no good here, so I'm going to shift you over here," you tell yourself about that person. Often, your failures, particularly emotional failures, fall along these lines: you create a situation for the person to do something to hurt you. You often repeat the same pattern in order to validate a theory you believe is true. Then, you sink back to the bottom of the self-pity pile, because that feels like the safest and most familiar place to be.

The greatest challenge is to live a life that gets it right. It is always dangerous to take on the role of the victim, because that denies you the chance to overcome the pain. Rather than blaming others for the wrong done to you, ask yourself, "I was mistreated, humiliated. Now, what am I going to do about it?" After all, it has already happened. Revenge and hurt cannot cure that. Nothing that happens will change your past experience. But you have the power to choose what to do with that experience—you really are in control.

Free will has nothing to do with what happens to you in life. No one consciously chooses to have cancer or dementia; no one consciously chooses to die in a car accident. Yet there is a belief that you choose what happens in life, as well as your father, your mother, your experiences, but in fact, the only thing you can choose is how you live those experiences. Whether you are unmoved or furious when someone you love dies, that person is not going to resuscitate. The experience happens and that's it. That person continues to be part of your life because of everything you shared with them. They are part of your life and always will be.

One way or another, you have to cross the transitional gap, the interval, the hiatus. Those who do not embrace this process of loss are unable to renew themselves for the next step. It is as if you were stuck in the birth canal. You have left one place, but refuse to arrive at the other. You have become stuck in the loss.

These small deaths are perhaps the most dramatic, because after they happen, you still go on, continuing to be fully aware of the loss. Embracing that pain is the best way to let it go. Is the relationship over? Then fully experience your mourning for the relationship. Did you lose your job? Experience the mourning for that loss. Experience the pain, live it, do not shy away from it, do not be cowardly, do not belittle the experience. If it was a twenty-five marriage, a thirty-year relationship, thirty years in a job, you cannot simply kill or eliminate all that time. When you enter into a new situation, the best way to live it is by thinking it is going to end. You have to live it intensely so that, when the time comes, you can say, "It was totally worthwhile! I left a legacy, I changed things. I will not be forgotten, I went all out to succeed, I went into that job giving my best, I went into the relationship giving my best."

What you have to bring with you from past experiences is the change they wrought in you. You do not carry the past with you, but the fruit of that past. And the past will only produce fruit if there has actually been an encounter, if you really have immersed yourself in it completely.

It is much easier to mourn a great love than a war. The most complicated mourning comes from ambiguous relationships, where there was love and hate, and which left a great deal of rough edges. When there is love, and death intervenes, it does not kill off the love. The love does not die. However, when it is a tragic story of a job where you took advantage of a lot of people, or spent night after sleepless night because of a project you did not like, then the mourning comes at far greater cost. You left some valuable things behind there: your good character, your good name, your sensitivity, your quality of life. When you are given notice, you think, *I paid a high price for all those years.* But when you lose a job you loved, that transformed you, where you grew and nurtured dreams, of course, that hurts, but you know it was worthwhile, because of everything you learned. That freedom, that lack of regret, projects you toward a world that is even more real and intense than the one you were living in.

The most loving recovery process is your own. Everything that can possibly be done is pure love when you are willing to be reborn.

CHOOSING HOW TO DIE: ELEMENTS OF A LIVING WILL

"'What is the most amazing thing in the world, Yudhisthira?' And Yudhisthira answered, 'The most amazing thing in this world is that, although everyone is dying, people think that they will somehow live forever.'"

Mahabharata

When doctor and patient talk about death, it is never easy. It is not unusual for that conversation never to take place, even when the patient is severely ill. Because I have worked in Palliative Care for many years, I have developed techniques for broaching the subject with patients and their families. In fact, I decided to write a guide for day-to-day use in my work. Working with a friend, who happens to be a great lawyer and has studied orthothanasia, I drew up a document of advance directives, or a living will. When I started to have these conversations in my surgical unit, I found if the subject was properly handled over two or three appointments, it was well received.

The first conversation is a solemn moment; it cannot be treated as routine. When we introduced this procedure at a large institution for older adults, we proposed adding four new questions to the admission interview. Although the script for that initial interview was nineteen pages long, it was quite common to find that all of the questions had been answered except those four, which were simply ignored. The first to object to these questions were the geriatrists themselves—"What will patients think if we ask them something like this?"—so they decided to add them alongside other, simpler questions about updating vaccinations and health histories.

The resulting sequence went something like this: "Are your vaccinations up to date? Have you ever had an operation? Do you smoke? Do you drink? Have you ever been admitted to hospital? If you have a heart attack, do wish to be revived?"

It was almost comical, as though we were talking about the elephant in the room, while pretending it was a fly on the window. Of course, this took a long time to decide—and meanwhile, the questions were simply left unanswered. This went on until the manager of the institution decided to hold an open talk for residents and their families on the subject of human mortality. That was the first talk I had given for lay people. I confess that it was one of the most incredible moments of my life: being approached by dozens of older people thanking me for my courage in speaking so clearly about something they had been needing so badly to hear. From then on, these questions were asked up front and were answered.

The conversation about advance directives, about what you want or do not want for the end of your life, should take place first among your family members, maybe at dinner or during Sunday lunch. For your safety and the safety of your older or ailing relatives, it is advisable that this conversation take place at a time when the disease is neither active nor progressing. It should happen in a normal family setting, and be framed almost philosophically, as what used to be called "having an important conversation."

Often it is not the palliative care doctor who will bring this up first. That initial approach is usually made by the clinician, geriatrist, or any other doctor preparing to make a diagnosis of a severe and incurable disease. However, as I mentioned, doctors get no training at medical school to help them have this important conversation with patients. They know how to talk about diseases, but not how to talk to sick people about their suffering. You do not learn to talk about death and mortality unless you specialize in Palliative Care. That means that 99 percent of doctors have no idea how to do it, because 99 percent of doctors are not going to specialize in Palliative Care and, even if they wanted to, there is still not enough support and guidance in Brazil for all the healthcare providers who haven't the slightest idea of what it means to provide care for dying well.

I think if society were to mobilize to make its wishes clear—and here I mean even culturally making people more aware and educated about this point in their own lives—that would perhaps make it simpler, in the future, to offer care designed to safeguard the dignity of the life of the person who is dying.

Here I want to outline the historical perspective of where we stand in Brazil as it pertains to Palliative Care. Our country is one that offers legal and ethical support for good Palliative Care to be practiced everywhere. We are the only country to have a Code of Medical Ethics in which "Palliative Care" is an option, written down in black and white. We have a federal constitution that favors the practice. We have the right to Dignity in Life. I have this conversation with my patients in Palliative Care and their relatives who are aware of their loved ones' wishes. In the patient's medical record, I describe the whole conversation, then offer them the document to read and leave them completely free to sign it with me there or not. On the medical prescription I write, I make it clear to the care team and my other doctor colleagues: "Patient has permission for a natural death."

When I write in the patient's record that I am doing all of this for Dignity in Life, I am putting Brazil's constitution into practice. Could I be taken to court? You can always be charged, but it is extremely unlikely you will be found guilty, because the basis of all medical conduct is communication. I respect my patients' autonomy; I responsibly take the greatest care that their suffering is minimized. I make it very clear that I do not practice euthanasia. Death will come, it will be accepted, but it will not be expedited.

Our Civil Code says that no one may be subjected to torture. Keeping a patient in the ICU with no hope of leaving there alive is torture. Subjecting them to painful, futile treatment is torture. Palliative care practitioners often fear they may be charged with murder. I understand murder as a situation where, if the crime had not been committed, the person would be alive. That is not the case with a patient at the terminal stage of a severe, fatal disease. The disease is going to kill them, not the care designed to minimize their suffering. We do not yet have laws that require people to live forever. Diseases kill and cannot be taken to court for that.

When you offer real Palliative Care, you are not hastening the patient's death. Palliative Care is completely different from euthanasia.

This kind of care is still not properly provided in daily practice at Brazilian hospitals. Doctors do not know how to provide care, so they eventually prescribe palliative sedation for nearly all patients in terminal suffering, even as palliative care professionals are working actively to have palliative sedation prescribed exclusively for conditions where the recommended treatment would cause more suffering.

Nowadays, palliative sedation is often prescribed for suffering where the expertise of the doctor isn't in Palliative Care. Doctors do not know how to provide care, how to medicate for the pain, or gasping respiration. They do not know how to work as part of a team so that their patients' existential and spiritual suffering are appropriately evaluated and alleviated. They prescribe sedation because they lack the necessary knowledge and skills and are unable to manage the dying process any other way.

Today, palliative sedation is prescribed excessively, and always too late. Patients suffer terribly for a long time and then, just before they die, they get sedation, as if it were a final act of compassion.

In Brazil, euthanasia and assisted suicide are prohibited. I have often been invited to join round table discussions at conferences as if I advocated these practices, but they are totally contrary to Palliative Care. I personally believe they are extremely complex, highly developed measures that cannot be put into practice in a country that is so immature in its attitudes and conversations about death. I do not perform or advocate them, because there is no room for euthanasia in Palliative Care. I accompany my patients until their death comes, and death comes at the proper time. I have no right to speed that process along, much less to delay it. To date, only a few people have asked me to cut their suffering short—and, in most cases, when the suffering was alleviated, they stopped asking to cut their lives short. They lived longer, lived as well as possible, lived and died with their suffering under control and with dignity.

The document I use in the unit as a living will has four important parts. It begins with a list of all the relevant information in Brazil's constitution, its laws, and Federal Medical Council regulations. And as I already mentioned, Brazil is a country that favors good practices regarding patient autonomy, something I made clear in the document. The second part of the document relays the choice around the "power of medical attorney," those people patients choose to represent their wishes. This does not necessarily need to be a legal representative, because it is the patient's choice that prevails here: the patient designates people close enough to them to know what their priorities are in this matter and who understand how they make decisions.

In the medical record, the patient's wishes must always be documented. It must be clearly stated that the document is being signed by a patient where there are no signs of depression, no cognitive deficit, nor any emotional pressure being exerted on the patient that might affect the decision process for these directives. Studies into directives for patients with dementia are ongoing in Brazil, but there is insufficient data available to allow incorporating them into living will directives. In such cases, what prevails regarding end of life care is family consensus. The greatest challenge facing geriatrists is how to approach the diagnosis of dementia with their patients at a time when they are still able to understand and make critical judgments about their future decisions. Even with a diagnosis of cancer in older adults, little is communicated regarding a living will and medical directive, so imagine the magnitude of questions and misinformation in a diagnosis of dementia.

Another fundamental point that needs clarifying is that these directives only apply when the person is dealing with an unquestionably incurable disease that causes them suffering or leaves them unable to lead an independent life. The patient can then declare, based on the principle of the inherent dignity and autonomy of every person, that they accept their life is ending and reject any extraordinary, futile intervention; in other words, any medical measure that will yield little to no benefits when weighed against potentially harmful effects.

My main recommendation when a patient wishes to draw up a document of this kind is that it should be drafted with their doctor. There is no way you can decide on medical interventions without a medical professional to explain in detail what each of the terms and options means. Drafting a document of that importance without proper guidance would be like choosing a meal from a menu in a foreign language and unknown alphabet, choosing a mystery meat when you thought you were ordering artichokes.

In the last section of the living will document, the signatory describes how they would prefer to be treated in matters ranging from day-to-day issues, such as bathing, diaper changes, and their living environment, to funeral arrangements; their wishes regarding organ donation, cremation, the wake, and so on may also be specified at this point.

The best way to feel confident about end of life care and limiting interventions is to talk about these things while you are alive and well. When you fall ill, this kind of conversation, however necessary, becomes a much more delicate matter.

The best way to feel confident about end of life care and limiting interventions is to talk about these things while you are alive and well.

LIFE AFTER DEATH: TIME FOR MOURNING

*"Suddenly, you were gone
from all the lives you left your mark upon."*

Neil Peart

More important than what happened in your life, is how you lived it or what you lived for. One of the biggest lessons I have learned from caring for people at the end of their lives is not to reply to "Why?" but to "What for?" "Why?" conjures up past motivations, while "What for?" projects you toward the future. What are you living this life for?

Suffering a loss can allow you to see the magnitude of love you were able to feel for someone, to realize how generous that person was in waiting for you to accept their death in your own time. When experiencing loss, you may finally understand who God is to you, what is sacred for you. You may finally learn whether you understood spirituality as something under your control or as something to which you surrender with humility.

The losses you suffer, especially the deaths of people you love dearly, may present a "What for?" question, but it can take quite a while before the answer becomes clear. The "Why?," meanwhile, will never have a satisfactory answer, even though you spend your whole life looking. No answer to that question can ever match the vastness of the experience of mourning. And I am not about to produce a new version of all that has already been written about mourning. What I will do is try to present a new perspective on a human experience as complex and final as losing a very important someone.

The first thing to be said is that the person who dies does not take with them the life history of those they shared their lives with and became important to. Absolute death, the disintegration of every dimension of a person whose existence had meaning in the lives of others, is an impossibility. Death concerns only the physical body. My father died, but he is still my father. Everything he taught me, everything he said to me, all that we shared lives on in me. Two truths arose that I have had to come to terms with since he died: first, he has become invisible; and second, there will be no shared future in our relationship. There will be moments when I will think about him, I will miss him a lot and, when I face problems ahead, I will remember advice he gave me. Then, depending on how I decide to mourn his death, I will know how to find him inside me during those experiences that the future holds for me.

The process of mourning starts with the death of someone who is very important in your life. That important connection is not always love alone, and the more it is contaminated by complex feelings like fear, hate, hurt, or guilt, the harder it will be to deal with the process. When a bond of genuine love is broken, there will be a lot of pain, but at the same time, that love will lead you to relief by the shortest route. The pain of mourning is proportional to the intensity of the love in the relationship ended by death, but it is also through that love that you are able to rebuild.

When I am caring for a mourning relative in great suffering, I try to make it clear how important it is to decide to focus on the value of their loved one's legacy. If that person brought love, joy, peace, growth, strength, and meaning into their lives, then it is not fair that all those things should be buried along with a diseased body. By understanding the value of the relationship, the mourning relative can begin to emerge from their pain.

The pain of mourning is proportional
to the intensity of the love in
the relationship ended by death,
but it is also through that love
that you are able to rebuild.

Technically, mourning is a process that follows the breaking of a significant bond. The experience of losing someone important robs you of the assumption you have cultivated that your world is stable and secure, your illusion of being in control. When you lose connection with someone important, forever, someone who represented a measure for your life and for yourself, it is as if you lose the ability to recognize yourself.

At no time in your life do you receive any kind of education on how to be who you are. As a child, you express the truth about yourself and about what you feel and think, but often your family, your school, and your society make you feel ashamed of your identity. Then you need other people's advice and insight on how to express yourself in the world, which is shaped by the expectations of others and the expectations you yourself create—or at least you try to be what the world around you would like you to be.

The biggest part of you is what others make you. You are molded by other people's perceptions of you. What you are going to miss most when someone important dies is how that person sees you, because you need other people in order to gauge who you are. If someone I love no longer exists, how can I know who I am? If I need other people in order to understand the world, and that other person is no longer there, what will the world be without them?

When someone you love and who is important to you dies, it is like being brought to the mouth of a cave. On the day of their death, you enter the cave, and the way out is not the same way you came in, because you will not find life the same as before. The life you will come to know after that death will never be the same as when the person you loved was alive. In order to leave that cave of mourning, you have to dig your own way out.

That is why we talk about "working through" grief—doing something active, building toward a new life. Digging your way out of a cave of mourning calls for action, strength, effort—and people in mourning often just feel intensely tired, existentially and physically. You cannot ask anyone else to enter the cave with you and dig your way out for you. It is during the mourning process that you will rebuild your own life—that is, rediscover its meaning—out of the loss of that very important someone.

Mourning is essentially a process of profound change. There are people who can make your time in the cave less painful, but they cannot do the work for you. The most delicate task in mourning is to reestablish connection with the person who has died through your shared experiences. Outrage, fear, guilt, and other feelings that contaminate the time of sadness ultimately prolong your time in the cave and can lead you to very dark places within yourself.

During a loved one's disease, you experience a kind of premourning in which you may find yourself thinking about what life will be like without that person. In this period of imagining loss, people around the patient may have wonderful opportunities to heal damaging emotions by working on forgiving, thanking, showing affection, caring. Genuine love between two people that is pure and full of truth lets go, sets free. Any other feeling should die with the body.

Everything you learn from the person who has died continues inside you. During mourning, if you devote yourself to healing the pain of bereavement, you will be able to clearly assess everything you experienced and all the good the relationship brought into your life. You may oscillate between two extremes. That oscillation, known as the "dual process" model of grief, was described by Margaret Stroebe and Henk Schut, recognized for their studies and writing in this field. There are moments in the dual grieving process when you are completely immersed in pain and suffering at the death of the person you love. At the other extreme, you are immersed in your day-to-day reality, dealing with everyday matters that may or may not be connected with the loss: donating the person's things, solving bureaucratic problems, such as closing bank accounts, disconnecting the telephone, taking inventory, and so on.

When the pain is extreme, it brings grief, tears, despair, and anger. All of these feelings must be accepted and experienced. When people ask me if they can cry, I say, "Yes, cry, but cry a lot. Really cry, a lot. Let your whole body cry until you shudder. Lie on the bed, kick and shout. Let yourself go, open yourself up, engage fully with the pain. Accept the situation." It's almost magical how, when you accept the presence of pain, you also experience the pain then going away. Meet the pain head-on, because it has someone's name on it. When you acknowledge that suffering, it nearly always diminishes. When you deny it, it takes over your whole life.

There is nothing wrong with being sad; it's a necessary part of any healthy mourning process. You may live under the false impression that you are supposed to be smiling and happy all the time, but sadness is perfectly acceptable. If the people around you keep telling you to get over it, you can understand that it hurts them to see you suffer. They do not know how to get you through this period, nor how they would react in your place, so they do everything they can to push your pain away.

Most people have no idea how to deal with the sadness of someone who has lost an important other, especially when the person's grief is still fresh. They want the mourner to go to a doctor right away and start treatment with antidepressants. They want the pain to be over quickly. Wrongly used, however, antidepressants or sedatives can envelop the mourner in emotional anesthesia, with devastating repercussions. These substances stop you from feeling pain, but they also deaden your ability to feel happiness. Sadness is not depression. During this time of extreme emotions, when the obligations of life nudge you to do normal, everyday things, there may also be happy, satisfying moments. The joy or success of a relative or other loved one could very well bring a smile back to the mourner's face.

The problem with our contradictory society is that it frowns on too much happiness during mourning, and mourners often feel guilty at finding reasons for wanting to smile in the midst of grieving. They ask me if it is normal to laugh and I say, "If it is a sad time, then laugh until you cry. You can even die laughing! It is okay to be sad to the last tear drop—and to laugh so hard you shake."

It does you good to remember how you laughed with the person who has died. When I meet with someone in mourning, I ask them to list all the good they learned from the person who died. Then I suggest they tell me about some of the funny moments they shared. With those two invitations, I see a beautiful process unfold before me, as the person in mourning reencounters their loved one in new ways in the midst of their pain. They nearly always talk about loss, disease, suffering, and death, but when I ask them to remember their life together—the good, intense, life-altering memories, I reintroduce the essence of that relationship. Through that conversation, I am able to show the person in mourning how the person who died left life full of meaning; after all, the lessons learned from their shared story never die. The mourner should never be deprived of their memories and feelings. Love does not die with the physical body. Love always endures.

If you have lost or are losing someone you love very much, try this exercise: list all of the things you learned from that person and then remember days when you laughed with them. When these memories make you laugh out loud, meditate on that. The tears you shed in that process will greatly ease your pain. Tears are made of salt water, like the sea. Crying from that bittersweet emotion is like bathing in the sea from the inside out.

Everything can die, except love. Only love deserves to stay alive forever within you.

"Things aren't all as tangible and expressive as people would usually have us believe; most experiences are inexpressible: they happen in a space that words have never entered, and inexpressible above all else are works of art, those mysterious existences whose life endures beside our own small, transitory life."

Rainer Maria Rilke

IN BRAZIL: CHANGES IN END OF LIFE CARE

"You'll see, no son of yours will run from the fight,
and those who adore you fear not death itself."

From Brazil's national anthem

In Brazil, we have been sluggish around the palliative care issue for nearly thirty years, as the results of early efforts to improve in this area of care only really showed up in 2011 or 2012. Health professionals who insist on offering Palliative Care in Brazil develop precious virtues like patience and determination as part of their daily medical practice, which entails sowing seeds that take forever to sprout. There is a lot of discussion over why Brazil is nearly thirty years behind the level of quality care found in North America and Europe. To give you a sense of the disproportionate lag, today there are about 180 palliative care services in Brazil, most of them public, while in the United States there are over four thousand.

Most justify the difference by talking about Brazil still being in its infancy as a country. But historically, our society is largely made up of the descendants of immigrants and native Brazilians of different indigenous nations, among whom there is profound respect for the preservation of their original culture. Immigrants came to Brazil in search of opportunities they could not find in their countries of origin. Fleeing from wars, starvation, slavery and death, they crossed the ocean to the enchantment of this "nearly" promised land, abounding with beauty, space, fertility. Here, they learned to imagine a happy life again.

Since coming to this land was a fleeing from death, that subject could not be allowed to take over their thoughts when building a life here. I think that is why nonindigenous Brazilians do not allow ourselves to bring up the subject of death. Those who stayed in their home countries knew that death comes, but that life prevails. Wars, recession, hunger all came, but so did reconstruction, renewed hope with each day of struggle, and persistence in the day-to-day rebuilding. Those immigrants who arrived in Brazil continued the legacy of keeping one's eye on the horizon, leaving no room for thoughts of death as the final outcome of human life. And so we go along, with our peculiarly Brazilian spin on things, claiming we're in control of difficulties and smiling as we evade problems.

That was how our humanity evolved as a large immigrant population, but the avoidance of death could not shield us from experiencing all the suffering entailed by diseases that have no respect for your body, your fears, or your loves. Diseases that threaten the continuity of life. Regardless of the origin of the person who falls ill, suffering will become a part of life and, unless it can be mitigated, the end will nearly always be horrifying.

The 2015 survey I mentioned earlier by the *Economist* ranked Brazil forty-second out of eighty-three countries in quality of death. Uganda, which only two years earlier had ranked lower than Brazil, overtook us, because it began testing public palliative care policies, which then led to developing Palliative Care, bringing it to a whole new level.

In 2016, continuing the tireless work of the team that preceded him, the Brazilian doctor, Daniel Forte, along with a team of committed partners, managed to secure nearly unimaginable gains from Brazil's federal authorities. After dozens of meetings, emails, open discussions, and a great deal of determination, finally, in 2018, the *Official Gazette* declared Palliative Care had become approved policy in Brazil. The state now stresses that Palliative Care is a necessity of society and an unrestricted right. Some 75 percent of Brazil's population, more than 155 million people treated by the national health system, will have access to this valuable, much needed care when confronted by a disease that threatens to end their lives. That is a veritable quantum leap toward excellence in Palliative Care in Brazil.

Without a doubt, Brazilian society is now more educated with better information regarding the need to think and talk about death while people are still in good health. Therefore, let us all, side by side, patients, relatives, society at large, set out for that veritable "promised land" that cares, saves lives, and protects from absurd and unnecessary suffering. Here in Brazil, we are capable of building something wonderful with Palliative Care and sharing it worldwide, because (as I have said so many times in my career) we have the unique enthusiasm of those who know how to live with a hope for better days. Our challenge, though, continues to be that we are a culture refusing to think, speak, or acknowledge emotions around death.

Let us all, side by side, patients, relatives, society at large, set out for that veritable "promised land" that cares, saves lives, and protects from absurd and unnecessary suffering.

A 2018 study to identify Brazilians' awareness of issues relating to death, commissioned by Brazil's union of private cemeteries and crematoria (Sindicato dos Cemitérios e Crematórios Particulares do Brasil, Sincep) and conducted by Studio Ideia, indicated constant interventions are needed to help make Brazilian society more receptive to conversations and understanding around questions of mortality.

One of the main findings in the study was that the subject is almost absent in daily life: 74 percent declared death was not an everyday topic of conversation. Brazilians also associated death with difficult feelings such as sadness (63 percent), pain (55 percent), loss (55 percent), suffering (51 percent) and fear (44 percent). Only a small number associated it with feelings outside the realm of anguish, such as acceptance (26 percent) and liberation (19 percent).

Interviewees acknowledged their difficulty in talking about the subject: on a scale of one to five (where one indicates "unprepared" and five, "strongly prepared"), Brazilians scored 2.6 for their readiness to deal with death; yet regarding their own death, the mean score fell to 2.1. Based on a sample of one thousand people, representative of Brazil's overall population, the survey showed that the older the respondent, the more present the subject of death was in their day-to-day discourse. The subject came up in conversation for 21 percent of the young people from eighteen to twenty-four years old; and for those over fifty-five, the percentage jumped to 33 percent.

One sign that the taboo around dying persists throughout life is that, despite differences between age groups, the percentages are all small. A significant portion of the interviewees regarded the subject as depressing (48 percent) or morbid (28 percent). I still get frequent messages from people upset by my habit of talking about death. They accuse me of being morbid and ask ironically if my talking about death gives meaning to my life. They even accuse me of being instrumental in bringing sadness into people's lives when I raise the subject. The anger in those messages reveals a lot about how they perceive death.

The survey also showed that Brazilians have reservations about how, and to whom, to talk about death: 55 percent agree that "it is important to talk about death, but people generally are not prepared to listen." There's a card game, Cards of the Sacred Choices (Cartas das Escolhas Sagradas), developed by the Associação Casa do Cuidar for use among people with advanced diseases who want to talk about what is important to them in the moment. The most common: "To be able to talk about what most scares me." I imagine the second would be "To have someone who listens." While this is an intimate subject for 57 percent of interviewees, a majority indicated friends and close relatives as the people they would most approach to talk about it.

Although the taboo is strong, no one escapes having to deal with dying at some point, either when they themselves are seriously ill or when someone very close to them dies. We still have a lot of work to do. The recent policy gains will certainly bring us closer to a more humane situation and better technical quality in the care offered to the seriously ill for their suffering. We must now embark on a major endeavor to train health professionals and build awareness of the need to talk responsibly and compassionately about dying.

Although scientific advances in Medicine have sequestered death to the inside of hospitals, almost like a kind of forbidden event, it needs to be returned to Humankind. We have the right to live—and to die—with dignity.

ACKNOWLEDGMENTS

It makes me so happy to be saying thank you; I have to smile at the scenes brought to mind by the many memories of the incredible, unimaginable moments I've enjoyed and shared over the years. Once again, and most importantly, I must thank Rogério Zé, who interviewed me for the TEDxFMUSP—and helped me believe that this idea of people thinking more about life in death could spread around the world. I thank Gustavo Gitti for his generosity in allowing our conversations about death to become the sweet seeds of this book. I thank Maria João for the wonderful invitation to write this book. I am very grateful to Pascoal Soto, an unconditional friend who always believed in the potential of this book to contain a proposal for a new "culture of care" in our world, regardless of cultural differences I am thankful for the patience and commitment of Sibelle Pedral in editing the text, and for wonderful moments fueled by cake, coffee, and so much inspiration. To my friends, especially Sonia, who is so good at celebrating my joys and blessing my fragilities. My parents, who now dwell in me, I thank you for my origin, my strength, and my determination. And on my children, Maria Paula and Henrique, I shower thanks for being such a loving presence in my life.

NOTES

LIFE IS MADE OF STORIES: HERE'S WHAT I DID WITH MINE

Excerpt translated from Ser *Mortal* by Atul Gawande copyright © 2014 Atul Gawande, Galaxia Gutenberg, S.L. Used by permission.

WHAT IS PALLIATIVE CARE?

Excerpt translated from Portuguese to English. Originally from "Global Atlas of Palliative Care at the End of Life" (Worldwide Palliative Care Alliance/World Health Organization, January 2014). Used by permission.

TALKING ABOUT DEATH, TALKING ABOUT TIME

Eugène Minkowski (1885–1972) describes three "dualities" of perspectives on time very well. Summary of dualities provided here, presented with permission.

THE SPIRITUAL DIMENSION OF HUMAN SUFFERING

Reference: "The Price of Your Soul: How the Brain Decides Whether to 'Sell Out,'" eScience Commons, January 22, 2012, a study/paper out of Emory University.

REGRETS

Reference: *The Top Five Regrets of the Dying: A Life Transformed by the Dearly Departing*, Bronnie Ware, Hay House, 209.

MAKING YOURSELF HAPPY

Summaries of ideas from *Os Quatro Compromissos,* Don Miguel Ruiz, Editora Best Seller LTDA, 2021, (English edition title: *The Four Agreements*). Used by permission.

LIFE AFTER DEATH

Reference: "The Dual Process Model of Coping with Bereavement" (DPM; Stroebe & Schut, 1999). Margaret Stroebe and Henk Schut, researchers on grief.

BRAZIL

Reference: A 2018 study commissioned by Brazil's union of private cemeteries and crematoria (Sindicato dos Cemitérios e Crematórios Particulares do Brasil, Sincep) and conducted by Studio Ideia.